CLOSE COMMUNION,

OR

OPEN COMMUNION?

AN

EXPERIENCE AND AN ARGUMENT.

BY

CRAMMOND KENNEDY.

NEW YORK:
AMERICAN NEWS COMPANY,
119 AND 121 NASSAU ST.

CONTENTS.

PREFACE.

As far as the method and subjects of water baptism were concerned, it was his reading of the New Testament when he was a boy that made the author a Baptist; but he became a close communionist by friendly administrations coated with logic, which he took for the pure article throughout, and which affected him for a long time, owing to the confidence which he had in their strength. When the hold of these arguments upon him was weakened, he did not consult any work on open communion; and when, after much feeling and meditation, his views were changed, and he decided to give them expression, he purposely avoided Robert Hall on the subject in hand. His admiration for him was great, but his desire to depict the very process of the change, to make his book subjective through and through, was greater. And, although the title came to him like a revelation,* neither did he read John Bunyan on the same side any further than his argument to show, that, if communion be one of the "all things" which disciples are to be taught to observe after immersion in water, and NEVER *at all if not after water baptism,* then love to God and one another, preaching and praying, "all things," indeed, "whatsoever" Christ has commanded, are so conditioned. This seemed to the author both awful and absurd, for it made him feel at once, that, if it were true, he was awfully and absurdly mistaken. But he did not know, that, by as much as we are quick to apprehend the relation which a statement sustains to our convictions or our prejudices, we are often slow to consider whether or not it be true. This disposition does not characterize the world of to-day so much as that of the past, for discoveries and inventions do not wait so long for a fair trial, and thoughts are judged rather by what they are than by the run of thinking before.

* "Differences of Judgment on Water Baptism no Bar to Communion."

The Author does not use the term "close communion" invidiously, but as a convenient name for the practice under consideration.

It will be noticed in his "Experience" that the main barrier which kept him from open communion was the doctrine of Indorsement. This was so because he then regarded water baptism as essential to the Lord's supper, and feared that he would sanction what he considered the double error of Pedobaptists in the method and subjects of the former, by inviting them to the latter, or partaking of it with them. It was not until he saw that the loving command of Christ, "This do in remembrance of Me," gave the requisite authority to all His disciples, and heard Paul's question, "Who art thou that judgest another man's servant?" with the conclusive rejoinder, "To his own master he standeth, or falleth," that he felt free to commune with fellow Christians, whom he considered, as far as water baptism was concerned, unbaptized.

At this stage he would have appreciated the noble apology which was made recently by Dean Alford for participating in the exercises of Cheshunt College, and thereby fraternizing with Congregationalists. "I claim to be," said this minister of truth, "as to every church doctrine, unchanged by fraternization with those who differ from us; and they, on their part, stand on the same ground. *On the firm maintainance of this principle all true recognition and union depend.*"

But a diligent study of the Scriptures has taken the Author beyond this liberty into the conviction, that, however appropriate may be the order which has prevailed in Christendom, the Lord's supper is not so connected with water baptism that submission to the one is necessary to the observance of the other.

Anticipating the objection which has been made before, that it is late in the day of the world and the church to intimate that any new lesson, so different from the ancient habit, is yet to be learned from the divine word, he replies that it will always be an inexhausted thesaurus, and that the jewels which have been worn by the bride of Christ for ages will ever sparkle with new combinations of colors in the unceasing and increasing light from God. That true pastor, John Robinson, knew well that the wisest and devoutest of his time, far less the pedants and the bigots, had not comprehended the sum of revealed truth, when he said to his flock, ere the Mayflower bore him and the new world from Leyden: "I charge you before God and His blessed angels, that you follow me no further than you have seen me follow the Lord Jesus Christ. *The Lord has more truth to break yet out of His holy word.* I cannot sufficiently bewail the condition of the reformed churches, who are come to a period in religion, and will go at present no further than the instruments of their reformation. *Luther and Calvin were shining lights in their time, but they penetrated not into the whole counsel of God.* I beseech you, remember it—'tis an article of your church covenant—that you be ready to receive whatever truth shall be made known to you from the written word of God."

Luther, too, who was free to use the argument from human authority when it suited him, had scarcely grace enough to receive it kindly from Rome; for in his commentary on Galatians he thus defiantly makes his complaint: "Even so the pope at this day, when he hath no authority of the Scripture to defend himself withal, useth this one argument continually against us, 'the Church, the Church.' Thinkest thou that God is so offended that for a few heretics of Luther's sect He will cast off His whole Church? Thinkest thou that He would leave His Church in error so many hundred years? And this he mightily maintaineth, 'that the Church can never be overthrown.' Now, like as many are moved with this argument at this day, so, in Paul's time, these false apostles, through great bragging, and setting forth of their own praises, blinded the eyes of the Galatians, so that Paul lost his authority among them, and his doctrine was brought into suspicion."

All that the Author has written to show that the Scriptures do not make water baptism a prerequisite to communion, is opposed to the creeds of Pedobaptists everywhere; and therefore it will be seriously misapplied if it is directed exclusively or mainly against the close-communion Baptists. It is for many others, and but few of them, that the chapter on "Water Baptism and Spirit Baptism Distinguished," is needed or intended.

However his zeal for his convictions may seem to contradict his profession, the Author is sure himself, and is anxious to have it believed by his kindred in Christ, that he speaks the truth, as he understands it, *in love*, and distinguishes between the close communionist, who is his brother, and the theory and practice which he is constrained to oppose. If he has written anything of another spirit, he hopes that it will be ascribed to the heat of the moment rather than the grain of the heart, for he counts it a sin, in view of the general discussion of the subject which is impending, and the probable denominational division, to say a word to weaken Christian love, or kindle a counter flame. Underneath and notwithstanding all our differences, this life from God doth still remain, and make us one, for it is the "Charity" which "never faileth," and of which it must always be said, though Faith and Hope be standing by, that "the greatest of these is Charity."

CLOSE COMMUNION,

OR

OPEN COMMUNION?

AN EXPERIENCE.

WHEN I joined the Baptists, I felt that I was in the midst of certainties. There was no doubt about anything. Calvin was infallible—except in his views of the method and subjects of baptism. I studied him more than his Master, and I looked at the Lord and all His revelations in nature and grace through this one man, and therefore I saw them "through a glass darkly." In preaching, I sometimes epitomized his teachings, as I understood them, thus: "God knows, and therefore has foreordained, how many, and who, of you will be saved. *You* will believe. The Spirit will help you. You cannot resist Him. The rest of you will be damned." I seldom dared to follow the same line of argument in the case of the unhappy part of my audience, but I knew that it was a short and plain road to the dread dark ending. Arminians, charitably speaking, were fearfully mistaken, and sadly deceived; and Fullerism was a dangerous compromise. Then I gloried in being a Calvinist; but another of the names borne by the different ideas which their subjects agree to call orthodox, had to be attached to me at my examination for ordination, when it appeared that I no longer believed in the Limited Atonement; and, so, a friend, who wanted me to pass, kindly dubbed me a Fullerite. A classification of opinions has its use, but when systems are so absolutely standards that reference is habitually made to them, differing, as they do, while the Word of God lies open, and the right of private interpretation is a fundamental of Protestantism, there is ample reason to suspect an abuse; especially when we feel that Christ is still with us, and is leading us into truth. It did not occur to me then, as it has so often and so painfully impressed me since, that in these names, and many others, by which Christians describe themselves, we may see how history repeats itself, and that the Church at Corinth was the prototype of a vast succession: "Now this I say that every one of you saith, I am of Paul; and I of Apollos; and I of Cephas; and I of Christ. Is Christ divided? Was Paul crucified for you? or were ye baptized in the name of Paul?"[1] In these days I believed in one baptism, and I believe in it now, but then it was always in water, and under it. To this water baptism the baptism of the Holy Ghost had invariably to be shaped. I was troubled that in Isaiah's prophecy of Christ's kingdom it should be said, "So shall He sprinkle many nations,"[2] and that Joel in recording the divine promise had been inspired to say: "I will pour out my Spirit upon all flesh[3];" but while wondering that cloven tongues of fire denoted the fulfilment, I was comforted because it came with "a sound from heaven, as of a rushing mighty wind, which filled all the house where they were sitting."[4] So anxious was I to have a bodily immersion, that sound would do instead of water or spirit, if nothing else was available. Close communion was a logical, if not a pleasant necessity. The logic seemed simple, clear, and conclusive. Baptism was a prerequisite to communion, nothing but dipping was baptism, and therefore none but the dipped could properly commune. It followed that Baptists should invite to the communion none but "members of sister churches of the same faith and order, in good and regular standing," and should commune with these

[1] 1 Cor. i., 12-15. [2] Isa. lii., 15. [3] Joel ii., 28. [4] Acts ii., 2.

only. Here it all was in a nutshell, and that was my palace, or my prison, as I chose to regard it. There was no escape from it, and wisdom would make the best of it. Of course I was wise, and magnified my position. I was standing up for a principle; yea, moreover, I was suffering for it, for not without pain I refused to sit at the Lord's supper with so many whom He loved, and who loved Him, as well as the disciple that leaned on His bosom. The longing for their presence was all very well, but obedience was better. If in remembering that the Master said, "Do this in remembrance of Me," I ever desired to do it with His disciples and my kindred in Him, outside of the Baptist churches, I was to fortify myself with arguments, and not to let my heart get the better of my head. That Christ was the vine, and believers the branches, that there was vital union among them here below, and that it would be perfect yonder, above, was true and most blessed, but not at all relevant to the question of communion. This was my heart again, and I knew that it was deceitful above all things, and desperately wicked. Yes, but even Solomon speaking for God had said: "My son, give me thy heart,"[5] and Paul had told us that "with the heart man believeth unto righteousness;"[6]

[5]Prov. xxiii., 26. [6]Rom. x., 10.

and all the preparation which the eunuch had needed for baptism was implied in Philip's answer: "If thou believest with all thine heart thou mayest."[7] So it appeared, that, after all, my heart was an important part of me in the fundamentals of religion, and I suspected that perhaps it ought to be heard on subordinates. But then, was I not under the most solemn obligations to protest against infant baptism, which was the "pillar of popery," and against sprinkling, which had never been substituted for dipping till the heresy prevailed that baptism was necessary to salvation, and parents had to choose between having their weak babies catch cold in the font, and leaving them liable, unbaptized, to death and damnation? If I communed with Pedobaptist Christians I would sanction and confirm them in these grave errors, which took them into an unscriptural communion and an unscriptural church. Sometimes I queried whether our celebration of the Lord's supper together would necessarily involve this deplorable result; and whether, if it followed, it would not be because we said it would. Were there no differences inside of our own denomination? Did I not indorse the doctrine of a General Atonement by partaking of the symbolic bread and wine with my

[7] Acts viii., 37.

deluded brother who held to that heresy? Why were the forms of water baptism and its administration to infants so vitally connected with communion that it indorsed them, and not other opinions and practices? The final appeal was always "to the law and the testimony," which meant the New Testament, and was made with so much confidence that my interpretations, and even my inferences, or rather those to which I was helped, were either identified with the authority itself, or relied upon as if they shared its inspiration. John's baptism was not only "from heaven," but it was also "Christian baptism;" all the Apostles were baptized; Paul did not rebaptize the Ephesian disciples, who had been baptized "unto John's baptism," but had not so much as heard whether there was any Holy Ghost; and apostolic example uniformly sustained close communion, despite the fact that as far as we know, Christians did not differ then about the form and subjects of baptism.

Although I settled down into this belief and practice, I was not always free from doubt. Whenever I felt that they who loved Christ were one family, and when I used to read the accounts of His institution of the Supper in the Gospel, I was troubled that I could celebrate it with none but Baptists.

Of course they were good enough company, but I yearned to see the faces of some others of my brethren as a sign that our Saviour's prayer for us was answered: "That they all may be one; as Thou Father art in me and I in Thee, that they also may be one in us; that the world may believe that Thou hast sent me."[8] But I was told that the fault was theirs, not ours, and that the ordinance did not express Christian fellowship. Still it was in remembrance of Him, and my heart could not see why His disciples might not thus remember Him together. The consideration that it was really in obedience to Him, and for their good—not in self-righteousness and exclusiveness, but in love and humility—that I refused to commune with them, had the most influence upon me, and kept me in the Baptist ranks. But almost as often as I partook of these most sacred symbols, I had to think over the reasons why I could not partake with other disciples—for instance with my mother. Not that this was the hardest case, for Christian experience had taught me somewhat of Christ's meaning when, in announcing the new law of relationship, "He stretched forth His hand toward His disciples and said, Behold my mother and my brethren! For whosoever shall do

[8]John xvii., 21.

the will of my Father which is in heaven, the same is my brother, and sister and mother."[9] "Yes," a Baptist friend might answer, "but that's just what the Pedobaptists do not do; it's the will of God that they should be immersed." If I rejoined: "This not only excludes them from supping with us, but also with the Lord both here and hereafter," I might be told that their failure in professing Him properly would be forgiven, but that we must guard His table till He set it in heaven.

I suspected then, and I think I see clearly now, that it was detrimental to my spiritual growth to be compelled to justify myself in communing apart—to consider, almost as often as I communed, the reasons why I should sit, as it were, at a separate table in a corner, while most of the family were keeping Thanksgiving round another board in the old homestead. In presence of these memorials I ought rather to have been thinking of Him, and how His love so joins all believers to each other and to Himself, that they are "His body, and members in particular."[10] And so I often did, but my thoughts of spiritual union had the striking and abnormal background of division, and of absence from the feast where Love presides, and where the past, with Christ's Cross

[9] Matt. xii., 49, 50. [10] 1 Cor. xii., 27.

and our sins, appears to grateful Memory, and the future, with His crown and our inheritance, to triumphant Faith. But I argued that communion was a church ordinance, and involved church fellowship, which we could not extend to those who were in error both as to the subjects and mode of baptism. This reasoning I believed to be sound, and that I ought to follow it, but it acted like a shower-bath on my heart. We all seemed to be sure, that, as far as the Scriptures were concerned, the case was settled, need I say, in our favor ; and I remember that although we professed to recognize no other authority, I yet was taught to make much of the fact that nearly all denominations regarded water baptism as essential to communion. I forgot just then, I suppose, how we stood in Christendom as to numbers on pedobaptism and sprinkling. When we are few, it is convenient to say that Truth is generally in the minority, but the quotation does not occur to us when it is our side that has the majority. In regard to the mode and subjects of baptism, I would accept no inferences, no probabilities, no analogies, from the Scriptures or elsewhere—nothing less than a plain, positive, thus saith the Lord ; but I dealt largely in inferential and hypothetical reasoning—much more than I was aware of then—when communion was the question. Consistency is a jewel which we are apt to lose when we are intent on establishing our case.

I did not know what to do with Hall, Spurgeon, Noel, and other lights among the open communionists. They were Baptists when I wanted to boast of the denomination, but outside of it, or a mere milk-and-water sort, when their practice was pitted against mine. As for John Bunyan, I thought he was the greatest Baptist of them all till I found on an old book-stand in Nausau-street, what had been dropped from "The Bunyan Library" in the hands of the American Baptist Publication Society—"DIFFERENCES OF JUDGMENT ON WATER BAPTISM NO BAR TO COMMUNION;" and as I had always seen Roger Williams put into our show-window when we wanted the world to see what a fine stock we had inside, I had taken it for granted that he was a "dyed in the wool, an out-and-out Baptist." I was so much of this sort myself, despite the misgivings which I have mentioned, such a TERRIBLE BAPTIST as Dr. Malcom said of himself at our last convention, that when I heard in London that many of our ministers from America communed in Pedobaptist churches while travelling, and gave out that they took a different course at home because their people were not ready for the more liberal practice, I could scarcely credit it, and avowed that I could not consistently commune even with open communionists; for if I would indorse pedobaptism and sprinkling by communing with Presbyterians, I would indorse the indorsement which they received from the open communionists, if I communed with them; or, at least, and this was surely enough, I would indorse them in indorsing the others! Fettered, as the Lord's Supper was to me with these implications and embarrassments, I had to look upon it, in common with American Baptists, as something belonging to each Baptist church in its individual capacity, but even in these narrow limits, as travellers would come to China, there was difficulty in making a consistent application of our doctrine of indorsement. For example: If I saw a man at the communion-table, in whom I had no confidence (alas that Judas is still among the disciples, and Simon still thinks that the Holy Ghost can be bought with money!), I was not to hesitaté to commune for fear of indorsing him. Why not? Because my communion was with Christ, and I was doing this in remembrance of Him, showing forth His death, "until He come." But if, as a deacon, I were distributing the elements, I must not hand them to Mr. Beecher, or even, according to the conscience of many of my brethren, to

Mr. Spurgeon, if either of them happened to be worshipping with us; because, in the one case, we would be indorsing pedobaptism, and (occasional) sprinkling, and, in the other, open communion, or what it indorses. Some of my Baptist friends held that they could commune with any Christian who had been immersed, but judging them by the then usual form of invitation, they were not orthodox, and if they had acted as they thought, the Church might have judged that they came within the scope of that apostolic injunction, which had special reference to "busybodies," who lived on the churches, and ate without working; namely, "Withdraw yourselves from every brother that walketh disorderly."[11] A minister, who had preached for Mr. Spurgeon, and knew him well, told me that he refused to commune in his church, and would not invite him to communion if an opportunity offered. To do this he would simply need to give the invitation which I have quoted.

How the expression of a fact changes with the student! He sometimes fancies that he is looking at something altogether different. But the difference is in himself. A Christian among Christians, who kept his seat with the intention of communing,

[11] 2 Thess. iii., 6.

was asked if he belonged to that church, or any other of the same order. Replying in the negative, he was informed that the members did not wish him to partake. "Oh," said this disciple, rising to go, "I beg your pardon, I thought it was the LORD'S SUPPER, but I see it is a *private entertainment.*" It seems strange that I could ever regard this as a jest, or doubt that the man might have honestly interpreted the Scriptures on this subject, and spoken out of an earnest heart, sharply touched in the tenderest spot. But, drinking in the spirit of by-gone battles (a sort of intemperance which is too prevalent in the churches), I had persuaded myself that Pedobaptists were not so anxious to commune with us, and did not feel so troubled at their exclusion, as they represented. I held that they would not invite us to their table if we did not exclude them from ours, and, indeed, that if we had not excluded them, they would have excluded us. It was just a game of bluff, at which we had been successful. This feeling, more of which may exist among us than we imagine, is simply the fomenting of the bottled theological wrath with which the contending sects have filled their cellars for us, their successors. But this is part of our inheritance, which we should reject, for the Present has sufficient sources of alienation to make it criminal to keep its channels open from the Past.

It was a satisfaction to know that, in communing, I did not indorse individual character; for, to say nothing about anybody else, I was not compelled to indorse myself, except as a sinner repenting of his sins, loving his Saviour, and being a member of a close communion Baptist church, "in good and regular standing," namely, not under church discipline. That this was a happy deliverance, will be granted readily by every one who has Christ for his ideal, and anything like an adequate sense of his own shortcoming.

But what shall I say of the moral effect of all this hair-splitting of the letter, which, being so intricate, and so differently viewed by my Baptist brethren in some of its minutest details, occupied so many of my thoughts, and so much of my soul? Sometimes, when, on looking inward and outward, the solemn import of life and the ministry weighed more heavily upon me, these words of the Lord came to me with some sort of relevancy: "Wo unto you scribes and pharisees, hypocrites, for ye pay tithe of mint and anise and cummin, and have omitted the weightier matters of the law, judgment, mercy, and faith."[12] I

[12] Matt. xxiii., 23.

fancied that my mind could hold just so much, and that if anything, by frequent thought and discussion, took more room than it ought, two evils followed,—first, the subject had more space than it deserved, and second, there was less room for the far greater valuables. So, as the balance still appeared to be in favor of close communion, I resolved, while finally accepting it, to give it few of my thoughts and words, and to have more to do with man as the sinner, God as the Father, and Christ as the Saviour. But the whole subject was brought up again on a memorable Sunday, at Baptist Noel's church, in London. Knowing something of his history, and of what sacrifice he had made of preferment in the National Church, and position in society, counting it as nothing, I was sure, that he might follow conscience and Christ, I listened with unusual prepossession to a sermon, so simple, so sweet, so humble and yet so grand, because so essentially Christian and Godly, that of itself it would have held me fast, and lifted me upward. I need waste no words in trying to express the unutterable emotions of a stranger in a strange land, who meets the Master among unknown disciples, in an unfamiliar place, which, by the divine enchantment of love, becomes "none other than the house of God, and the very gate of heaven." The preacher closed, and as I bent my head to join in his prayer, I saw by the furnished table that the Lord's supper was to follow and to crown the service. But not for me. The battle between my doubting, longing, and unsatisfied heart, and my poor, misinformed and prejudiced, but still faithful head, was renewed, with more wounding and confusion than ever before; and I left the scene—the inviting Saviour, His inviting minister, His inviting disciples, and the inviting emblems of His body and blood, the very bread and wine seeming to beckon me forward—and, like an alien, I passed out of the sanctuary, with the dying request of Jesus sounding in my ears: "DO THIS IN REMEMBRANCE OF ME." I think that the doctrine of Indorsement received its mortal wound in one of the pews, and expired in the porch, of that plain old meeting-house, which is hallowed by a good man's ministry. I never rested till I sat by the table on which, with a mistaken fidelity, I had turned my back. How ridiculously scrupulous, and presumptuous, too, the doctrine of Indorsement appears to me now! I know in my heart whether I indorse a thing or not, and I have a tongue to express my opinions at proper times and in fitting words; but then, in fear of indorsing what I considered minor errors, by sitting at the Lord's table with fellow disciples, I used to go about the world, and into churches, the veriest fraction of the people, if any, knowing either who I was, or that I was there, and far less what I thought about the method and subjects of water baptism.

In the light that came to me after the partition wall of Indorsement had fallen, I was better able to judge my action in another test to which my views of communion had been put in Edinburgh. I had returned to my native land, which I left for the new world as a wee laddie, and was invited to preach to an Independent church that had no minister. Not knowing that they were in the habit of communing every Sunday (here is an example for rigid literalists to consider), I gladly consented, and preached on the opening words of the Lord's prayer. My subject being the Fatherhood of God, and my residence in a distant country, I naturally dwelt gladly on the family that was growing up in every kindred, and tribe, and tongue, into the likeness of His Son, and into the Heavenly Home. But imagine my horror when my eye rested on the cloth that covered the bread and the wine, which my brothers and sisters in the Lord, some of them my parents' friends in auld lang syne, were expecting to partake with me in the spirit of my sermon. I did not know what to do, and wished we were all Quakers. I did not think it would be proper for me to explain my position ; I could not conscientiously serve at the table ; and so I pronounced the benediction, and went to the vestry. Here the deacons met me, and, thinking I was unwell, expressed their concern, and wanted to know how they could help me. But I had an affection of the heart, which, as I saw by their faces, they could scarcely understand, far less cure. So when they had told me that there was no other minister present to officiate, and had heard my poor explanation, and regrets, they let me go. What a position it was for a Christian minister to occupy in a land where Baptists were few and divided ; or indeed, wherever he might labor outside of his own sect! I could preach in the Established Church of Scotland, wear a gown and bands, and give out the "psalms of David in metre," without indorsing the union of church and state, ritualism, or the literary character of the Hebrew bard as he appears in English doggerel; but if I ate and drank with these Presbyterians at the Lord's table, I at once became a party to their views of baptism! Not long afterward I was invited to preach to an Independent church in Dundee, but this time I took the precaution to inform them that they must have somebody else in readiness to preside at the communion—an announcement, which, I am afraid, did not better the services to the hearers who were aware of it. Since the time when Indorsement, that old enemy of my peace, was slain, I have often wished for an opportunity to share the memorials of our Saviour's death with these fellow-Christians from whom my former convictions kept me aloof.

It is easy to hold a theory which is not put to the test of practice at every point of application. Hence it is, I think, that so many continue committed to close communion. They seldom are absent from their own church ; and if they are, they are generally in reach of one of the same faith and order. They therefore hold to their exclusiveness as Dr. Brown held to the dogma that there is no natural good, till he was saved by a wicked crew from perishing of cold. The story is charmingly told in "Spare Hours." The venerable preacher had a distant appointment, which, as usual, he was bent on keeping. But when the day arrived, the wind was high, the snow was falling fast, and his friends were urgent that he should postpone his visit. Yet go he would ; and before he was half way he was chilled and blinded by the increasing storm ; his carriage wheels were clogged ; and his pony, a beastie that had seen better days—being very tired, and finding it hard to pull on snow balls, tumbled over, and rolled into the ditch with his load. The snow was deep, the mercury low, and but little blood in the old man's veins. There he lay at the white icy door of death, when who should come along but these roughest of characters—Scotch carters with whiskey. They see the wreck in the drift, draw out the puir wee body, bring him to with the chafing of hands made horny with toil, but which human kindness yet makes tender, wrap him up in their plaids, and gie him a wee drappie from one of the barrels to warm him inside. Repenting of his hard thoughts of his fellows, and full of gratitude for his deliverance, the old man uncovers his head, gives thanks to Heaven, and asks a blessing on the cordial he is about to take, and on his preservers, the reckless neer-do-weels that stand around, and watch him with moistening eyes. Experience taught him wisdom; and at the first succeeding convention of his ministerial brethren he told them how he had found the better side of bad men, who, even at the worst, have somewhere upon them a fingermark of God. If Dr. Brown had not fallen in with such characters in some such circumstances, he would probably have died with a different and a darker understanding of those scriptures which refer to human depravity. Had I settled early as a pastor, and been altogether with my own particular flock, they might have confirmed me, and I them, in close communion, but the nature of the thing would not have been fairly tested. I suppose that this accounts for the alleged disorderly walk of some American Baptist ministers abroad.

I was brought closer to the embarrassments of close communion in Great Britain, but I had felt them at home ; for, as chaplain of a regiment in which most of those who bore the Christian name were Roman Catholics and Presbyterians, I not only was unable to commune myself, but I also prevented others from communing, to whom communion might have been a means of grace. They knew that, as a Baptist, I had conscientious scruples against intercommunion, and never proposed what, of course, I could not suggest. Yet, many a time before and after battle—the dreadful conflict and mortal danger impending through sad and loving thoughts of home ; or the struggle over, and the soil still moist on the upturned faces of our fallen comrades—we might have shown forth the dying of the Lord together, and strengthened ourselves with thoughts of our immortality in Him. But the Jordan seemed to me to flow by the Lord's appointment between them, and His table, at which I, who had "come up out of the water" was sitting, a welcome guest; and I could not commune with them, because in crossing the stream they had not gone under it. It is easy, and may be considered conclusive, to say: "You ought to have instructed them in the way of the Lord more perfectly;" which means that I should have convinced them that nothing but immersion was baptism, and that it was essential to scriptural communion; but surely, at such a time, it would have been unwise to discuss forms, especially in view of the difficulty of bringing many minds to one opinion. This difficulty, this serious inevitable fact, which met me so often, and which I once was so hopeful of reversing, had no small influence in forcing me, through church teaching, to the Lord Himself for an answer to two questions, which seem to me to be so intimately connected that they are essentially one: Am I bound to commune with Baptists only? Should none but Baptists commune? Ringing through the New Testament, interpreting and harmonizing all its teachings on this subject, and freeing the table from many of the burdens which the churches have put upon it, I heard my reply from the Eternal Word, the Way, the Truth, the Life: "Do This In Remembrance of Me."

THE LORD'S SUPPER
AS INSTITUTED BY HIMSELF,
AND
WHO ARE THE WORTHY COMMUNICANTS.

AND as they were eating, Jesus took bread, and blessed it, and brake it, and gave it to the disciples, and said, Take, eat; this is my body. And He took the cup, and gave thanks, and gave it to them, saying, Drink ye all it; For this is my blood of the New Testament which is shed for many for the remission of sins. But I say unto you, I will not drink henceforth of this fruit of the vine until that day when I drink it new with you in my Father's kingdom.—Matthew xxvi. 26–29.

And as they did eat, Jesus took bread, and blessed, and brake it, and gave to them, and said, Take, eat; this is my body. And He took the cup, and when He had given thanks, He gave it to them: and they all drank of it. And He said unto them, This is my blood of the New Testament which is shed for many. Verily I say unto you, I will drink no more of the fruit of the vine until that day that I drink it new in the kingdom of God.—Mark xiv. 22–25.

And He took the cup, and gave thanks, and said, Take this, and divide it among yourselves: For I say unto you, I will not drink of the fruit of the vine, until the kingdom of God shall come. And He took bread, and gave thanks, and brake it, and gave unto them, saying, This is my body which is given for you: this do in remembrance of me. Likewise also the cup after supper, saying, This cup is the New Testament in my blood, which is shed for you.—Luke xxii. 17-20.

For I have received of the Lord that which also I have delivered unto you, That the Lord Jesus the same night in which He was betrayed took bread: And when He had given thanks, He brake it, and said, Take, eat; this is my body which is broken for you: this do in remembrance of me. After the same manner also He took the cup, when he had supped, saying, This cup is the New Testament in my blood: this do, as oft as ye drink it, in remembrance of me. For as often as ye eat this bread, and drink this cup, ye do show the Lord's death till He come.—1 Cor. xi. 23-26.

John, the Evangelist, says nothing to indicate that Christ established an ordinance for His church when He ate the passover with the twelve, unless He ought to be understood literally, and as speaking to all His disciples, when He said, after washing the Apostles' feet: If I then, your Lord and Master, have washed your feet; ye also ought to wash one another's feet. For I have given you an example, that ye should do as I have done to you."[1]

This Gospel, however, which is silent on the breaking of the bread, and the drinking of the wine, contains the only record of words like those by which the Saviour made the last supper His memorial till time should end. Pitying the hungry multitude

[1]John xiii., 14, 15.

that followed Him, He gave thanks, and distributed "five barley loaves and two small fishes," among His disciples, who fed the wondering thousands therewith, and afterwards filled twelve baskets with the fragments.[2] Then, perceiving that they would take Him by force to make Him a king, "He departed again into a mountain Himself, alone."[3] From this solitude He walked in the love and power of God to the ship that His disciples were rowing in a great wind, a heavy sea, and a dark night, toward Capernaum.[4] Here the crowd that had sought Him on the other side, asked Him in surprise, "Rabbi, when comest Thou hither? and He replied, "Ye seek me, not because ye saw the miracles, but because ye did eat of the loaves, and were filled. Labor not for the meat which perisheth, but for that meat which endureth unto everlasting life, which the Son of Man shall give unto you."[5] It has been suggested that the walking on the sea occurred in connection with Christ's mysterious sayings about His body, in order that he might be understood not in the material sense, but in the spiritual. Then said the Jews to Him: "Our fathers did eat manna in the desert, as it is written, 'He gave them bread from heaven to eat;'" and Jesus answered, "Moses

[2] John vi., 9–13; [3] verse 15; [4] verses 16–19; [5] verses 26, 27.

gave you not that bread from heaven; but my Father giveth you the true bread from heaven; for the bread of God is He which cometh down from heaven, and giveth life unto the world.[6] * * Verily, verily, I say unto you, *He that believeth on me hath everlasting life.* I AM THAT BREAD OF LIFE. Your fathers did eat manna in the wilderness, and are dead. This is the bread which cometh down from heaven, *that a man may eat thereof and not die. I am the living bread which came down from heaven: if any man eat of this bread, he shall live forever: and the bread that I will give is my flesh, which I will give for the life of the world.*"[7]

"The Jews therefore strove among themselves (some of them, perhaps, suspecting a spiritual meaning) saying, How can this man give us His flesh to eat?"[8]

Then Jesus said unto them, Verily, verily, I say unto you, *Except ye eat the flesh of the Son of Man, and drink His blood, ye have no life in you. Whoso eateth my flesh, and drinketh my blood, hath eternal life, and I will raise him up at the last day.*"[9]

It seems impossible to doubt that there is a vital spiritual reality underlying these words—nothing less, indeed, than the very mystery of partaking of

[6]John vi., 31–33; [7]verses 47–51; [8]verse 52; [9]verses 53, 54.

the divine nature, and of union with God through Christ thus formed within us—and that this is identical with that which the communion symbolizes, and is. For the Saviour who said of Himself: "I am that bread of life," said afterwards of the bread which he blessed and brake at the last supper, "Take, eat; this is my body." He said also of Himself, "Whoso eateth my flesh, and drinketh my blood, hath eternal life;" and once subsequently of the cup, "Drink ye all of it, for this is my blood of the New Testament which is shed for many for the remission of sins."

It seems to me that the truth which He intended to convey, is, that we should feed upon Him, and live by Him, as a personal Saviour, as the Son of Man, too, as well as the Eternal Word, His humanity being represented by His flesh and His blood; or, in other words, that we, whom He makes kings and priests unto God,[10] should subsist upon Him as our voluntary atoning sacrifice, as our real Passover,[11] and our living Redeemer.

"For warm, sweet, tender, *even yet*
A present help is He,
And Faith has still its Olivet,
And Love its Galilee.

[10] Rev. i., 5, 6. [11] 1 Cor. v., 7; and Ex. xxix., 32, 33; Lev. vi., 16–18, 29; vii., 6–10 for the eating of the sacrifices by the priests.

"The healing of His seamless dress
Is by our beds of pain;
We touch Him in Life's throng and press,
And we are whole again."

The time came when some of the Jews, who had stood aghast at the idea of eating His flesh, and drinking His blood, received a better understanding of these mysterious and seemingly impious words,[12] which made many even of His disciples exclaim, "This is a hard saying, who can hear it?"[13] For, in full view of His death and resurrection, Peter uttered again that memorable confession of His Master, but this time to a different audience, and with a far richer meaning: "Therefore let all the house of Israel know assuredly, that God hath made that same Jesus, whom ye have crucified, both Lord and Christ."[14] Then, when they looked on Him whom they had pierced, whose flesh, as it were, they had eaten, and whose blood they had drunk, in their fury, they were pricked in their hearts, and constrained to inquire, "Men and brethren, what shall we do?"[15] Surely, when Peter pointed to Jesus as their Redeemer, and the darkness of their ignorance and unbelief began to melt in the brightness of His rising, and He Himself to beam upon them as

[12] Lev. vii., 26, 27. [13] John vi., 60. [14] Acts ii., 36; [15] verse 37.

David's Son and Lord, as their Brother, their Prince, and their Saviour ; surely, when they thought of Him who had taught in their streets, who had gone about doing good, who had spoken as never man spoke before, who had wept over their Jerusalem, and who, by their wicked hands, had died outside the gate for their redemption, surely with a hungry eager love they ate His flesh, and drank His blood again,—they took Him to their hearts as one with them, aud worshipped Him as God manifest in the Flesh, the Lord of Life, and the King of Glory. This appropriation of the Saviour to the soul is, as we shall see, the preparation for tho Lord's supper, as it is for water baptism.

It should never escape us that what we secure by eating the flesh and drinking the blood of the Son of Man, we obtain *by believing on Him.* "He that believeth on me hath everlasting life—ζωὴν αἰώνιον." "Whoso eateth my flesh, and drinketh my blood hath eternal life—ζωὴν αἰώνιον."

The body and blood of the Lord are symbolized by the bread and the wine of communion ; and our feeding on Him, and our union with each other, by our outward use of the same symbols. This is the symbolical significance of the Lord's supper. But it is more than a symbol, for, in the communion, the soul acts, and is acted upon, as well as the body. The Christian's celebration of the ordinance involves the spiritual process described by Christ to the Jews.

We should feed richly on Jesus always; and we may; for He says to us as He said to the twelve, "*Abide* in me, and I in you;"[16] but knowing that we are prone to starve ourselves, He has wisely and graciously ordained a reminder of Himself, and of our dependence on Him. "This is my body which is given for you; this do in remembrance of me."

Not only does the ordinance show the Lord's death, but it also suggests and fortells His coming, and His Father's kingdom, in which, and world without end, His flesh will still be meat indeed, and His blood drink indeed, in the same spiritual sense, to all His disciples.

The Lord's Supper has still another feature which by no means should be overlooked. The union of believers in Christ seems to lead naturally in the New Testament to their union with each other. When He said, "I am the vine; ye are the branches,"[17] He declared Himself to be the living, the life-giving, and the eternal Uniter of His people to Himself, and to one another. In His prayer for His disciples—not only for those who followed Him then,

[16] John xv., 4; [17] verse 5.

but also for them that should believe on Him through their word—how He binds them to Himself, to each other, and to God. "That they all may be one; as Thou, Father, art in me, and I in Thee, that they also may be one in us, that the world may believe that Thou hast sent me."[18] In the inspired mind of the Apostle Paul, thoughts of the Lord's supper awakened thoughts of the union of saints. The two were just as closely connected, in his estimation, as cause and effect; for, after teaching that the cup of blessing, which we bless, is the communion of the blood of Christ, and the bread, which we break, the communion of the body of Christ, he adds immediately, "*For we being many are one bread, and one body, for we are all partakers of that one bread.*"[19] No turning or twisting can alter or evade the truth which Paul so emphatically states, that just because the communion is feeding upon Christ, it expresses, and it is, the union of believers to each other in Him. But the Apostle gives it still a deeper meaning, for his words involve the very idea of identity. It is as if he had said, Partaking of that one bread, which is the body of Christ, is feeding upon Him; and we who eat the bread which we break, are thereby one

[18] John xvii., 20, 21; [19] 1 Cor. x., 16, 17.

bread, and we who feed upon the body, which was broken for us, are thereby one body.

Returning now to that prayer which the Saviour offered between the Passover and the Crucifixion, we hear Him saying, "Neither pray I for these alone (who communed with Him), *but for them also which shall believe on me through their word; That they all may be one; as Thou, Father, art in me and I in Thee, that they also may be one in us.*" Putting these scriptures together, I am as sure that the Lord's supper belongs to all those whom He thus describes, and thus bears on His heart to His Father, as I am that He loved me and gave Himself for me. Eighteen centuries are full of proofs that we cannot agree in our views of church organization and government, of days, of ordinances, and doctrines, but still, and none the less, the host of believers have always been, are now, and will be forever ONE,—"the body of Christ and members in particular;"[20] "in whom," to change the figure, and reiterate the precious truth, "all the building fitly framed together groweth unto a holy temple in the Lord."[21] The scriptures thus show that the Lord's supper is not only a sign, but also a means, of this oneness of

[20] 1 Cor. xii., 27. [21] Eph. ii., 18-21.

believers, which arises from their eating the same spiritual food; namely, Christ, their Life.

In explaining the communion to the Corinthians, who were carnal and schismatical, who abused the sacred memorials for gluttony and drunkenness, Paul delivered this solemn exhortation, "Let a man examine himself, and so let him eat of that bread and drink of that cup. For he that eateth and drinketh unworthily, eateth and drinketh damnation* to himself, NOT DISCERNING THE LORD'S BODY."[22] "*For this cause*," he continues, "many are weak and sickly among you, and many sleep." The preparation, then, for the ordinance, is inward, not outward. Our fitness is not in water baptism, and our unfitness is neither in our sprinkling, nor in our entire freedom from baptismal water. But, if we recognize the Lord in the bread and the wine, if we discern His body, if we feel that even we were meant when He said, "This is my body, which is broken for you," if it is true of us that "BY ONE SPIRIT are we all baptized into one body,"[23] Christ gives us the right, and will give us the blessing, of eating and drinking at His table.

Under the heading of "THE LORD'S SUPPER—*The proper method of its observance*,"—Lange's

*Appendix (1). [22] 1 Cor. xi., 29, 30; [23] xii., 13.

Commentary, in perfect unison with the words of Him who instituted the ordinance, and with Paul's exposition of its nature, teaches as follows: "The words 'given for you'—'shed for the remission of sins'—are associated with the act of eating and drinking the elements as expressing the chief thing in this sacrament; and *he who truly believes in these words is a right-worthy and well-qualified communicant.* But he who does not accept their truth, or doubts them, is unworthy and disqualified; for *all that the words 'for you' require is a sincere believing heart.*"

"Still further," continues this excellent chapter, laying hold of the apostolical idea of the union and identity of believers with each other by feeding on Christ in the communion,—"in my associates I behold One who is in *them*, even as He is in *me*, who imparts Himself to *them* as He does to *me*, who loves *them* as He does *me*, and who is beloved by *them* as He is beloved by *me*. Thus all sense of estrangedness is removed, and a feeling of true brotherhood is awakened, and a communion established wherein we freely share with each other what we have received from Christ."

But see what we American Baptists have made the Lord's supper, in connecting it as we do with our understanding of water baptism, and as neither Christ nor His Apostles ever connected it—a Baptist supper, at which, if this union, this identity, of believers in Christ, is realized and fostered, it logically extends to Baptist believers only ; for in this country the Baptist invitation to Christ's table, is to "members of sister churches *of the same faith and order.*" If the Baptist churches in America accept Paul's doctrine of the communion, that "we, being many, are ONE BREAD, and ONE BODY, for we are all partakers of that one bread," then, according to the Baptist invitation, and the Baptist conscience of who should partake, it is a Baptist bread that is partaken, and a Baptist body that results. This, it seems to me, is either schism, or, at least, depriving the commnnion of that very feature which grows naturally out of feeding on the Body and Blood of Christ—I mean the spiritual union, and sameness in kind, of all those to whom His Flesh is meat indeed, and His Blood drink indeed. That Christ intended the communion to symbolize and to have this effect, and that Paul portrayed this feature in the most positive and graphic style, it seems impossible to deny. True it is that the creeds of Christendom make water baptism in one form or another essential to communion ; but surely this is not a plea for our mouths who boast so often that we are not governed by human authority, but by divine. And then, as these other churches have the three gates of sprinkling, pouring and dipping, they are at liberty to welcome each other, and would gladly sit with us, at the Lord's supper ; while we having but the one gate of immersion, with indorsement for the key, are compelled to have a table for ourselves. We may be bold enough to say it is the Lord's, and the only one He has ; but our brethren, and may be the Master Himself. think differently.

There is not a word about water baptism in the Scriptures to indicate that it is an essential condition of participating in the Lord's supper. "This is my body," "eat ;" "this is my blood," "drink ;" "this do in remembrance of me,"—the One and only Saviour of "them that shall believe on me through their word." "He that believeth on me (mark the absence of water baptism in this connection) hath everlasting life. I am that bread of life. * * * As the living Father hath sent me, and I live by the Father, so he that eateth me, even he shall live by me." "Whoso eateth my flesh, and drinketh my blood, hath eternal life." "The cup of blessing which we bless, is it not the communion of the blood of Christ, and the bread which we break, is it not the communion of the body of Christ?" This too in a double sense, both relating to Christ Himself, on whom believers feed, and to them who themselves are His body; "FOR (the ὅτι holding on to what precedes) we being many are ONE BREAD and ONE BODY." Why? and How? "Because we are all partakers of that one bread."

Showing how American Baptists are compelled to ignore, or deny, this scriptural and natural meaning and effect of the proper celebration of the Lord's supper, a venerable minister was lamenting to me recently that it had ever been called *The Communion*, because, said he, it makes many think that we commune with each other, as well as with Christ! That this narrowing of its significance, this destruction of the harmony and fullness of its teaching, is common among us, I am an ear witness, and more, for the ordinance was once thus dwarfed and distorted to me. I think, too, that I see the explanation. If, say we, the Lord's supper were intended at once to illustrate and foster the union and identity of all believers with each other, in feeding on Him, our invitation is too exclusive. If this were Christ's design, who saw the end from the beginning, He would not have made participation in the ordinance absolutely dependent on previous water baptism, according to our understanding of it. But as he has, say we (and here is the *petitio principii*), our invitation is proper, and the Lord's supper neither shows that all believers are "one bread and one body," nor helps to make them so.

Taking the other view, that it *does* thus show and help, we are led to a position in which few are content to stand; namely, that believers, who have been baptized in water as water baptism is understood by Baptists, and that those believers only, are "the body of Christ, and members in particular." I say few accept this conclusion, and I doubt that any can, in view of Paul's declaration that "by ONE SPIRIT are all we baptized into one body."*

"It is clear from this passage," says Neander, "that Paul considers the unity of the church not as something formed from without, but as fashioned from within."

The Lord's supper, then, belongs to that body of which He is the Life. And that body is composed

* In examining the nature of the Lord's supper, the 11th and 12th chapters of 1 Cor. should be studied together, for, by applying what he says of the physical body to the Corinthians as "the body of Christ," in the latter, Paul joins it to his exposition of the communion in the former.

of all believers on Him, for "*he that believeth on the Son hath everlasting life.*"[24]

This is the argument from Scripture which has satisfied me, by making me feel that I have reached the heart of the matter, and that all other questions and difficulties are side issues which can, and must, be solved. For if we are persuaded that we apprehend the spirit, or, rather, are apprehended by it, we may expect to find a straight path through all seeming complications of the letter. Yea, if we have the spirit we have the solution of the letter, for, when brought into contact, they do not disagree. It is when we separate them, and make more of the letter than the spirit, that we are caught in the former and kept from the latter. It is better, then, to travel to the letter by the spirit, than to the spirit by the letter. But most take the longer and harder road, and become, like the Jewish scribes* and Judaizing teachers, servants, not of the spirit, but of the letter; "for the letter killeth, but the spirit giveth life."[25]

[24] John iii., 36; also verses 14–18; v., 24; vi., 29, 35, 40, 47; vii., 38; xi., 25, 26; xiv., 12. *Appendix (2). [25] 2 Cor. iii., 6.

THE BAPTISM OF THE FIRST COMMUNICANTS.

ALTHOUGH the Lord kept His last Passover, at which He instituted the communion, with none but the twelve Apostles,[1] yet He had far more disciples than these ; for the Scriptures tell us that He appointed other seventy also, who returned again with joy, saying that even the devils were subject to them through His name ;[2] that the Pharisees heard that He made and baptized more disciples than John ;[3] that certain women, Mary, Susanna, Joanna, and many others, who ministered to Him of their substance, were with Him, and the twelve, in His first tour of Galilee ;[4] that there were men who had companied with the Apostles all the time that He went out and in among them ;[5] and that He was seen of over five hundred brethren at once before His ascension.[6] It is probable that some of these followers had received baptism from those disciples who baptized, but none of them, although it is likely that they believed on Jesus as the Christ who had come, and whom they

[1] Matt. xxvi., 20; Mark xiv., 17; Luke xxii., 14. [2] Luke x., 1, 17. [3] John iv., 1, 2. [4] Luke viii., 1-3. [5] Acts i., 21, 22. [6] 1 Cor. xv. 6.

knew in person at the time of their baptism, partook, or were present, at His supper.

On the other hand, there is no record of the baptism of the first communicants.

Andrew, who was a disciple of the Baptist, heard him say as Jesus walked by, "Behold the Lamb of God," and, after going home with Him, brought Peter to see Him, and receive a new name. From the modest way that John the Evangelist has of speaking of himself, it is generally agreed that he was the other of the two disciples who heard the Baptist speak of Christ, and immediately changed Masters. The day following, Jesus findeth Philip, who afterwards finding Nathanael asked him to "come and see."[7] Another call was given to Andrew and Peter; and James and John were also called from their nets to be "fishers of men."[8] Matthew, sitting at the receipt of custom, heard Jesus saying "Follow me," "and he arose and followed Him."[9] Taking Nathanael to be Bartholomew, we have no account whatever of the circumstances of the calling of the remaining five—James and Judas, the sons of Alpheus, Simon Zelotes, Thomas, and "the traitor."

It is a fair inference, however, that Andrew and John, being disciples of the Baptist, had been bap-

[7] John i., 35–51. [8] Matt. iv., 18–22; [9] ix., 9.

tized when Jesus called them ; but it does not appear that there is a strong enough foundation for the positive assertion of the baptism of the others, then, or subsequently. Jesus did not baptize them, for He, Himself, baptized nobody.[10] It is not written that Andrew, or either of the two Johns baptized them ; and the objection, that these ten baptized others, being unbaptized themselves, applies equally to the Baptist. Although he claimed to be sent of God to baptize with water,[11] yet we must not overlook the indication that water baptism was no new thing to the priests and Levites, who said to him, "Why baptizest thou, then, if thou be not that Christ, nor Elias, neither that Prophet?"[12] They were not surprised at the act itself, but at its performance without such a character as entitled him, in their estimation, to institute a new order.* He seems to have regarded his baptism as a prophecy in symbol. "*I* indeed have baptized you with *water*, but *He* shall baptize you with the *Holy Ghost*;"[13] and Christ Himself made the corresponding contrast between the Baptist's disciples and His own: "For John truly baptized with water, but ye shall be baptized with the Holy Ghost."[14]

[10] John iv., 2; [11] i., 33; [12] verses 19–25. *Appendix (3).
[13] Mark i., 8, and parallels. [14] Acts i., 5; xi., 16.

Coming as he did in the spirit and power of Elijah,[15] and being declared by his Lord to be "Elijah, which was for to come,"[16] the Baptist answered to the descriptions, and fulfilled the prophecies, which were written aforetime concerning him. Belonging to the old dispensation, his work was none the less preparatory for the new. He was the voice of one crying in the wilderness, and he made straight in the desert a highway for our God; but he did not live in the city that began to rise where his axe was laid to the root of the trees. There was none among them that had been born of woman greater than he, but yet he was less than the least in that kingdom of heaven,[17] which he proclaimed as at hand.[18] "His whole mission," as Olshausen well observes, "was calculated, in accordance with the office of the law which gives the knowledge of sin,[19] to bring men's minds into that state in which the Redeemer invites them, as weary and heavy laden, to come to Him."[20]

What was John's formula in baptizing, if he had any at all, is not recorded; but simply that he preached the baptism of repentance for the remission of sins.[21] His baptism signified reformation[22] and remission, but not "the washing of regeneration and

[15] Luke i., 17. [16] Matt. xi., 14; [17] xi., 11; [18] iii., 2. [19] Rom. iii., 20. [20] Matt. xi., 28. [21] Mark i., 4. [22] Matt. iii., 8.

renewing of the Holy Ghost, which is shed on us abundantly through Jesus Christ our Saviour."[23] Why, then, did He who needed no pardon, because He had committed no sin, submit Himself in this rite to His forerunner? "Suffer it to be so now (as yet), for thus it becometh us to fulfil all righteousness."[24] He had not publicly proclaimed Himself, nor had He been attested by His Father, as the Messiah.[25] Moreover He was "made under the Law,"[26] all the righteousness of which He had fulfilled in His outward, as well as in His inward life; for He was circumcised on the eighth day,[27] and presented in the Temple on the fortieth;[28] He was subject to His parents,[29] and did not enter on His public ministry until He was thirty years old.[30] He doubtless also intended to recognize and sanction the Baptist as His predicted Messenger. But the appropriateness and significance of His baptism are seen most clearly in the necessity which was upon Him, as the Saviour of Man, "in all thing to be made like unto His brethren,"[31] Gentiles as well as Jews, and especially if the appearance of guilt were

[23] Tit. iii., 5. [24] Matt. iii., 15. [25] John i., 33. [26] Gal. iv., 4. [27] Luke ii., 21; [28] ii., 22; Lev. xii. [29] Luke ii., 51. [30] This ὡσεὶ τριάκοντα admits of considerable latitude, but only in one direction; viz., *over* thirty years.—*Alford's Greek Test;* Luke iii., 23; Num. iv., 3, 23, 43, 47. [31] Heb. ii., 17.

involved (witness His death,[32] and the form in which He suffered it), for He, who knew no sin, was made sin for us.[33]

The idea, however, that John's baptism was Christian baptism, *because Christ submitted to it*, is refuted by that very fact. What a singular argument it is which supports its conclusion by the very reason which proves it mistaken! It was Christ—not John—who established Christianity. And Christian baptism is both an institution, and an illustration, of established Christianity. Not of Judaism waning, nor of Christianity crystallizing, but of Christianity crystallized. Christian baptism, by its very name, draws its meaning and takes its character from Christ—from Christ alive, from Christ dead, from Christ buried, and from Christ risen. Hence it was that He did not give the Apostles their commission to baptize till after His resurrection. It was when Paul, in looking backward, saw behind his baptism the freighted cross, and the empty sepulchre, that he wrote to the Romans, "Know ye not that so many of us as were baptized *into Jesus Christ* were baptized *into His death?* Therefore we are buried with Him by baptism into death, that *like as Christ was raised up from the dead* by the

[32] Rom. v., 12. [33] 2 Cor. v., 21.

glory of the Father, *even so we also should walk in newness of life.*"[34] Peter, too, knowing well the difference between repenting and believing, calls baptism "the answer of a good conscience toward God, BY THE RESURRECTION OF JESUS CHRIST."[35] It is clear, that, as Jesus sanctioned it, John's baptism must have been of God's appointment, and therefore obligatory in its place; but it could not be Christian when the Author of Christianity found it, and submitted to it, *before He had shown Himself as the Christ*, unless, indeed, there were two Christs, and ours was the younger, or second in the field. To such lengths will some theologians go who have a case to prove which they have already decided.

Thus we have two conclusions, the proofs of which should be examined more in detail,—

(1.) John's baptism was not Christian baptism.

(2.) The baptism of the disciples, previous to the resurrection, was not Christian baptism.

Under the first head there are three things that appear from Scripture; (*a*) that John belonged to the legal dispensation; (*b*) that he had administered most of his baptisms before he knew Jesus as the Messiah; and (*c*) that he never became one of Christ's disciples.

[34] Rom. vi., 3, 4. [35] 1 Pet. iii., 21.

(*a*) The Baptist was by birth a Jewish priest, and by divine purpose and calling a prophet and a Nazarite. He was a prophet by the announcement of Gabriel ;[36] he was a prophet by his father's prophecy concerning him ;[37] he was a prophet by the call which he received from God ;[38] he was a prophet by his own declaration ;[39] he was a prophet in the estimation of the Jews ;[40] and he was a prophet, and more than a prophet, by the testimony of Christ.[41] He was "more than a prophet," inasmuch as he was the subject of prophecy, the messenger of the Messiah, and an eye witness of His attestation as such by the Father.

No greater prophet had been born of woman, yet the least in the kingdom of heaven was greater than he. This was said of him by Christ, after He had answered the question which was brought to Him by John's disciples from their master in prison: "Art thou He that should come? or look we for another?"[42]

Coming down from the Mount of Transfiguration where He had talked with Moses and Elijah, Jesus told His disciples not to tell the vision to any man

[36] Luke i., 17; [37] i., 76; [38] iii., 2; 1 Kings xii., 22; 1 Chron. xvii., 3; Jer. i., 1–4; Ez. vi., 1; vii., 1. [39] John i., 23. [40] Matt. xiv., 5; xxi, 26. [41] Matt xi., 9. [42] Matt. xi., 2, 3.

till He was risen from the dead. "Why then," they replied, "say the scribes that Elijah must *first* come?" Having just seen him for a few moments, and been enjoined to secrecy, they could not see how this prophecy had been, or could be, fulfilled. But Christ's answer set them at rest: "Elijah is come already, and they knew him not, but have done unto him whatsoever they listed;" for then they understood that "He spake unto them of John the Baptist."[43]

It was in the Old Testament sense that the Baptist was a prophet—not in the New. He was the last representative of the Law; and on this account the more intensely legal. Coming as he did from the desert, wearing camel's hair and a leathern girdle, and living on locusts and wild honey, he looked like the Law. His appearance and habits were severer than his Divine Successor's, who, Himself, has drawn the contrast: "John came neither eating nor drinking, and they say, He hath a devil. The Son of Man came eating and drinking, and they say, Behold a man gluttonous and a winebibber, *a friend of publicans and sinners.*"[44]

The call of the Baptist was like that which had come to his fellows throughout the dispensation

[43] Matt. xvii., 1-13; [44] xi., 18, 19.

which he closed: "The word of God came unto John the son of Zechariah, in the wilderness."[45]

His preaching too was of the legal kind. Morality was his theme. To the publicans he said, "Exact no more than that which is appointed of you;" to the soldiers, "Do violence to no man, neither accuse any falsely, and be content with your wages;" and to the multitude that came forth to be baptized of him, "Bring forth therefore fruits worthy of repentance."[46] There is more of the Gospel in the Prophecy of Isaiah than in the preaching and prophesying of John. But he was adapted, as he was sent, to awaken conscience by applying the law to daily life, and thus "to make ready a people prepared for the Lord." But that preparation was by no means of such a kind that all who submitted to his baptism believed subsequently on Christ.

The position that the office and ministry of John belonged to the legal dispensation is not weakened by those sayings ascribed to him in the fourth Gospel (granting that they include the last six verses of the third chapter), but rather confirmed; for they were uttered after he had baptized Jesus; and they distinguished their author's position from that of the

[45] 1 Kings xii., 22; 1 Chron. xvii., 3; Jer. i, 1–4; Ez. vi., 1; vii., 1. [46] Luke iii., 7–14.

least of those who were to know the Lord in His death and resurrection: "He that *hath* the bride is the bridegroom; but the friend of the bridegroom, *who standeth and heareth him*, rejoiceth greatly because of the bridegroom's voice: *this, my joy, therefore, is fulfilled.*" "Thus the parallelism," says Alford, "is complete: John not inferior to any born of women—but *these, even the least of them*, are born of *another birth.*[47] John the nearest to the King and the Kingdom—*standing on the threshold, but never having himself entered; these*, ἐν τῇ βασιλείᾳ, subjects, and citizens, and indwellers of the realm, ὧν τὸ πολίτευμα ἐν οὐρανοῖς.[48] He, *the friend of the bridegroom*, they, however weak and unworthy members, *His body and His Spouse.*"

Sad and yet most beautiful it is, that when the faithful and fearless Baptist was troubled with doubt in Herod's dungeon, Jesus used the words of another prophet to enlighten and comfort him.[49] Thus Isaiah strengthened John for his martyrdom, and helped to prepare him for the fullness of that blessing, which belongs, says Christ, to "whosoever is not offended in me."

[47] John i., 12, 13; iii., 5. [48] Phil. iii., 20, with *country, kingdom,* or *citizenship,* instead of "conversation." [49] Is. xxxv., 5, 6, (see also xi., 1-6; lxi., 1-3) compared with Matt. xi., 5.

(*b*) Elizabeth, the mother of John, and Mary, the mother of Jesus, were related and intimate. During a visit of the latter to the former, after the Annunciation, most wonderful and memorable communications passed between them. The people, too, "throughout all the hill country of Judea," not only heard of the wonders which attended the birth of John, but also 'laid them up in their hearts."[50] And the shepherds, when Jesus was born, "made known abroad the saying that was told them concerning this child."[51] The two children, therefore, doubtless heard of each other from their mothers, or neighbors. But, despite the Holy Families of the painters, it is probable that they never met till they were men. At all events, Jesus was known to John, who evidently held Him in great veneration; for, when He came to be baptized, the Baptist forbade Him (διεκώλυεν—motioned Him away with his hands), saying, "I have need to be baptized of Thee, and comest Thou to me?"[52] But we are not to suppose that John was sure at that time that Jesus was his Successor, for he says, "I knew Him not (as the Messiah), but He that sent me to baptize with water, the same said unto me, Upon whom thou shalt see the Spirit descending and remaining upon Him, the

[50] Luke i., 65, 66; [51] ii., 17. [52] Matt. iii., 14.

same is He which baptizeth with the Holy Ghost."[53] Until this time, therefore, neither John, nor any whom he baptized, knew who the Christ was.

At what period, then, of the Baptist's ministry, did he baptize Jesus?

The fourth Evangelist says, that when "John was not yet cast into prison," Jesus went with His disciples into the land of Judea, and that He tarried with them there, and baptized; also that the Baptist was baptizing in Enon, near to Salem, at the same time.[54] Still, it appears from the context, that his influence was waning, and that his work was closing; that he knew that this was his case, and accepted it cheerfully. Matthew says, that "from that time (the imprisonment of John) Jesus began to preach;[55] Mark, that "Jesus came into Galilee preaching the Gospel of the kingdom of God, after that John was put in prison;"[56] and Luke that the baptism of Jesus took place "*when all the people were baptized.*"[57] In Paul's sermon at Antioch, he speaks of God raising a Saviour unto Israel "when John had *first preached before His coming* the baptism of repentance to *all* the people;" and adds, that *as* "*He fulfilled his course*, He said, Whom think ye that

[53] John i., 33; [54] iii., 22–24. [55] Matt. iv., 12–17; [56] Mark i., 14; [57] Luke iii., 21.

I am ?"[58] In the house of Cornelius, Peter declared that the Gospel "was published throughout all Judea, and *began* from Galilee, *after* the baptism which John preached."[59] It is clear from these passages that Christ was among the last (Luke makes Him the very last) whom John baptized ; and that the Baptist's ministry had virtually closed before the Messiah's began.*

The Author of the Epistle to the Hebrews, who was certainly contemporaneous with the Apostles, inquires : "How can we escape if we neglect so great salvation, which *at the first began to be spoken by the Lord* (not by John), and confirmed unto us by them that heard Him ?"[60]

(*c*) It is beyond a doubt that the Baptist never became a follower of Jesus, for each in his lifetime, and after his death, had his own disciples. We find also that the followers of the two Masters differed. Matthew says that John's disciples came to Jesus, saying, "Why do we, and the pharisees, fast oft, but thy disciples fast not ?"[61] Mark gives the same as this in substance,[62] but Luke a version which involves other differences : "Why do the disciples of John fast oft, and *make prayers,* and likewise the

[58] Acts xiii., 24–25 ; [59] x., 37. [60] Heb. ii., 3. * See Appendix (7). [61] Matt. ix., 14. [62] Mark ii., 18.

disciples of the pharisees, but Thine *eat* and *drink*?"[63] Christ's answer indicates another, and a much more important difference, which does not seem to have entered the minds of His questioners: "Can ye make the children of the bride-chamber fast (thus distinguishing His disciples from John's), while the bridegroom is with them?"[64] (thus distinguishing Himself from him who may be said to have cried, Behold the Bridegroom cometh!)

It appears that but few of the many that John baptized attached themselves to Jesus as the Messiah. Positive mention is made of only two who joined Him while on earth from the Baptist! It is true that when He delivered His discourse on His forerunner, "all the people that heard Him, and the publicans, justified God, being baptized with the baptism of John;"[65] but there is too much reason to believe that many of their voices subsequently swelled the cry that was fatal to their nation and their souls —"Crucify Him! crucify Him!"

There seems to have been considerable rivalry, and even jealousy, between the two followings—mostly, however, on the part of John's. This is indicated by the questions which have been quoted already, and still further by the spirit in which they brought

[63] Luke v., 33; [64] v., 34, 35; [65] vii., 29.

the news of Christ's success to their master: "Rabbi, He that was with thee beyond Jordan, to whom Thou barest witness, *behold, the same baptizeth, and all men come to Him.*"[66] It has been supposed, but, I think, without foundation, that it was to make his disciples believe on Christ, that John sent a deputation of them from prison to ask Him: "Art thou He that should come, or do we look for another?"[67] The Lord's reply may have conduced to this end; but it is evident, therefrom, that whether John had expected miraculous deliverance from Herod, or had grown impatient at the delay of Jesus in proclaiming Himself the Messiah, or had been deceived by Jewish views of His kingdom, the doubt and the question were his own. "*Go and show John*"[68] was the direction of Christ's answer. The Baptist had previously made to his disciples an emphatic and evangelical confession of Jesus as the Messiah, and the Saviour of the world; and now the Lord crowns His forerunner with a eulogy of truth and love to brighten that cloud under which he passes from our view.

Still the influence of the Baptist was great, and his teachings concerning Christ were not forgotten. Apollos, who was an eloquent man and mighty in the

[66] John iii., 25, 26. [67] Matt. xi., 3; [68] xi., 4.

Scriptures, was instructed in the way of the Lord, and being fervent in the spirit, he spake and taught diligently the things of the Lord, *knowing only the baptism of John.*[69] The disciples that Paul found at Ephesus had believed, but *having been baptized unto John's baptism,* they had not so much as heard (*did not so much as hear* when they received baptism) whether there was any Holy Ghost; and therefore, they wishing it, Paul had them baptized in the name of the Lord Jesus.*[70] We find here in this re-baptism, which closes the mention of the Baptist in the Bible, a striking proof of the conclusion to which any one of our three steps inevitably leads us; for surely, if John's ministry and office belonged to the Law, or if he had administered most of his baptisms before he knew Jesus as the Messiah, or if he were not a disciple of the Christ, but the head of a separate following, his baptism was not Christian baptism. Then it follows, that without Christian baptism, and by express invitation of the Lord, Andrew, and John, the Evangelist, partook with Him of the First Communion.

(2.) The only record which we have of Christ's disciples as baptizers, previous to the resurrection, is found in the third and fourth chapters of John's

[69] Acts xviii., 24, 25; [70] xix., 1-7. * Appendix (4).

Gospel. Here we see that these baptisms were administered in Judea, before the Baptist's imprisonment; and, therefore, before the preaching of Christ, "which began from Galilee *after the baptism which John preached*," or, as Mark has it, "*after that John was put in prison*."

We have no ground for supposing that these baptizers were the twelve Apostles, for they had not yet been called. It is true that John, Andrew, Peter, Philip, and Nathanael, had already conversed with Jesus, and it is probable that all of them regarded Him thenceforth as the Messiah; but we find that the first three had resumed their occupations when He called them, by the sea of Galilee, to be His followers.[71]

In the charge which He delivered to the twelve to prepare them for their first mission—instructions which made the tenth chapter in Matthew's twenty-eight—He gave them no authority to baptize, although He entered into such details as what they should and should not take for their journey. And the same is true of His charge to the seventy. It ought also to be considered that He limited their efforts to "the lost sheep of the house of Israel," although He was the Saviour of the world, and for-

[71] Matt. iv., 18–22.

bade their entry into "any city of the Samaritans," although He had previously revealed Himself to these very people, and "many" of them had believed on Him "for the saying of the woman."[72]

Moreover, He instructed the twelve to preach, as the Baptist had done, that the kingdom of heaven was at hand;[73] and it is recorded of them, that, like him, "they went out, and preached that men should repent."[74] *From the time that they were called till the day of Pentecost, there is not a single baptism recorded. Indeed baptizing is mentioned in connection with believing but once in the Gospels*, and in that case after the resurrection.[75] Their only outward act was anointing with oil,[76]—one example, among many others, which we do not follow, although we foolishly claim to be literally, and alone of all the churches, apostolical.

Every student of the Gospel must have noticed how often Jesus showed anxiety to conceal those very things which seemed best adapted to prove His divine character, and command appropriate worship. Thus, as we have seen, He told His disciples that they should not tell of His transfiguration "*till the Son of Man were risen from the dead*;"[77] and when

[72] John iv., 39. [73] Matt. x., 7. [74] Mark vi., 12; [75] xvi., 16; [76] vi., 13; [77] ix., 9.

He gave sight to the blind,[78] when He opened the ears of the deaf, and loosened the tongue of the dumb,[79] when He healed the leper,[80] when He raised the dead,[81] *and when Peter confessed Him as the Christ,*[82] He straitly charged and commanded them to tell no man that thing. How, then, can we suppose that he had authorized any of His disciples to baptize in His name, as this very Christ, the Son of God, and the Redeemer of the world? In the prayer which He taught them, He made no allusion to Himself; and it was almost when His hour had come, that He added the plea through which the prayers of Christendom have since ascended to heaven: "Hitherto ye have asked nothing in my name: *ask, and ye shall receive, that your joy may be full.*"[83]

But the Apostles themselves did not understand either His character or His mission. Even John, who leaned on His bosom, mistook the nature of His kingdom, when he and his brother prayed that one of them might sit on His right hand, and the other on His left, when He should come in His glory.[84] Their mother also had made the same mistake, for Matthew represents her as making this request for

78 Matt. ix., 30. 79 Mark vii., 36. 80 Matt. viii., 4. 81 Mark v., 43. 82 Luke ix., 21; Mark viii., 30. 83 John xvi., 24. 84 Mark x., 35-40.

her sons.[85] But Jesus replied, "*Ye know not what ye ask*," and then He tried to show them that the heavenly glory comes by suffering—the Crown by the Cross. The Apostles were Jews, and thought of Jesus as a Jew. Nathanael confessed Him as the Son of God, but also as the *King of Israel*.[86] When He alluded to His coming resurrection, "they kept that saying with themselves, questioning one with another, what the rising from the dead should mean."[87] When He foretold His Passion, "Peter took Him, and began to rebuke Him, saying, "Be it far from Thee, Lord."[88] How He must have felt what depended on "the decease which He should accomplish at Jerusalem," when He replied to the Rock, and the Holder of the Keys, "Get thee behind me, Satan!" After He was dead, they did not expect Him to rise, and when He had risen, and appeared to the faithful women, "their words seemed like idle tales, and they believed them not."[89] Even after He came to them from the grave, and they knew Him, His disciples inquired, "Lord, wilt Thou at this time *restore the kingdom unto Israel*?"[90] No wonder that He upbraided them for their unbelief,[91] and said to two of them, "O fools, and slow of heart,

[85] Matt. xx., 20–28. [86] John i., 49. [87] Mark ix., 10. [88] Matt. xvi., 22, 23. [89] Luke xxiv., 1–11. [90] Acts i., 6. [91] Mark xvi., 14.

to believe all that the prophets have spoken. Ought not Christ to have suffered these things, and to enter into His glory?"[92]

We have seen that Paul's idea of baptism, and Peter's also, after the descent of the Spirit, involved the death and resurrection of Christ, and the burial and rising again of believers with Him. But the baptisms which we have been considering were administered while He was in the flesh, and before the administrators understood that He should die, and be raised again the third day. It is nonsense to talk, in this connection, about foreseeing and appropriating faith, for they did not want Him to die. It was by His life, not by His death, that they hoped His kingdom would come, and the subjects of their baptism were no wiser than they. Peter, who would have fought for Him with the sword, denied Him when He was captured; and "THEN," when He needed them most, all the disciples forsook Him and fled."[93] After He was crucified, they said of themselves, "We *trusted* (alas for the tense!) that it had been He which should have *redeemed Israel*."[94] It was to the risen Christ, whom they did not recognize, that they made this confession. "THEN *opened He*

[92] Luke xxiv., 25, 26. [93] Matt. xxvi., 56. [94] Luke xxiv., 21.

their understanding, that they might understand the Scriptures;"[95] *and* THEN *He gave them their commission to preach the Gospel and baptize.*[96]

[95] Luke xxiv., 45. [96] Matt. xxviii., 19, 20; Mark xvi., 15, 16.

APOSTOLIC EXAMPLE.

I CANNOT see how any careful reader of the Acts of the Apostles can believe that the primitive churches were intended to furnish an exact model in constitution, government, doctrine, and custom, for all Christians to the end of time—such an illustrated lesson as Moses had when he was instructed to make all things according to the pattern shown him in the mount. Certain it is that no church of the present day corresponds precisely with the first congregations. An exceedingly clear and conclusive proof of this statement is the fact that the first congregations represented to some extent the differences which existed among the Apostles themselves.

Christianity, both as an experience and an organism, grew. As an experience, it wrought in individual character, and through its circumstances, while, in its turn, is was modified and individualized by them ; and, as an organism, it was affected by the age on which its effect was so divine. The influence of Judaism on the Apostles, and that of heathen philosophy on the fathers, were far greater, and are much more distinctly marked in their histories, than is commonly supposed.

Christ in man is a growth. So is Christianity in the world. When Andrew and Philip told Jesus that the Greeks who had come to worship at the feast, wished to see Him, He made the seemingly irrelevant and mysterious reply concerning Himself and His Kingdom: "Verily, verily, I say unto you, Except a corn of wheat fall unto the ground and die, it abideth alone; but, if it die it bringeth forth much fruit."[1] He sowed Himself in human life, which, like a field, by the sky and the plow, had been prepared for Him by all the world's experience previous to His coming. With such seed below, and such a heaven above, eighteen hundred years have not passed in vain; and the present is richer by far in spiritual wealth than the past. That knew Him in the flesh, and holds His tomb; this knows Him in the flesh no more, but in the power of His resurrection, in His word abiding in us, and in His personal presence with us, "even unto the end of the world."

Christ is still growing in His Church, and His Church is still growing in Him.

Although the disciples had seen the risen Christ,

[1] John xii., 24.

and He had opened their understanding, and they had received the gift of the Holy Ghost, yet they still looked on the Saviour and mankind with Jewish eyes. The Gentiles could be converted, for proselytes were numerous; but their conversion was still to be to Moses and the Law, as well as to Christ and the Gospel; and circumcision was to be at once a condition and a sign of their reception by the Jewish Christians. Peter, who opened the door of the kingdom of heaven to the Jews (as he did subsequently to the Gentiles in fulfilment of the saying of Christ), spoke on the day of Pentecost, and in Solomon's Porch, and before Annas the High Priest, as a Jew. There are many expressions in these speeches which show the height to which his inner life had grown, and from which he looked on the world. Stephen seems to have been the first of Jewish believers to see the temporary character of the Law and the Temple; "for," said his accusers, "we have heard him say that this Jesus of Nazareth shall destroy this place, and change the customs which Moses delivered us."[2] How wonderful that he thus anticipated the Pharisee who "was consenting unto his death!" Saul little dreamed that the murdering zealots, who laid their clothes at his feet,

[2] Acts vi., 14.

were stoning his forerunner. During the persecution which this martyrdom inaugurated, "they that were scattered abroad," "travelled as far as Phenice, and Cyprus, and Antioch, preaching the word *to none but unto the Jews only.*"[3] Necessity was driving them where Christ had told them to "go," but still they did not know Him well enough to offer Him "to every creature."

In process of time, and most opportunely (for Paul had appeared as the Apostle of the Gentiles, and might have made a schism between the circumcision and the uncircumcision), Peter saw just such a vision as was fitted for a believing Jew whom Heaven intended to teach the way of the Lord more perfectly.[4] He was such an apt pupil that he went with the men whom Cornelius had sent, and preached to him, his kinsmen, and his friends, although it was unlawful for a Jew "to keep company or come unto one of another nation." But, although they received the word of God readily, the circumcisers contended with the preacher when he returned to Jerusalem, saying, "*Thou wentest in to men uncircumcised, and didst eat with them.*"[5] This same Apostle, who, as has been truly said, was the first to apprehend a great principle, and the first to draw back from it,

[3]Acts xi., 19; [4]x., 9–18; [5]xi., 3.

was subsequently opposed by Paul, who charged him with hypocrisy in this matter as follows: "And when Peter was come to Antioch, I withstood him to the face, because he was to be blamed. For *before that certain came from James, he did eat with the Gentiles* (and probably communed with them) but *when they were come, he withdrew and separated himself* (also, no doubt, from the Lord's table) *fearing them that were of the circumcision.* And the other Jews *disembled likewise with him,* insomuch that Barnabas also was carried away *with their dissimulation.* But when I saw that they walked *not uprightly according to the truth of the Gospel,* I said unto Peter, *before them all,* If thou, being a Jew livest after the manner of the Gentiles, and not as do the Jews, *why compellest thou the Gentiles to live as do the Jews?*"[6]

Well might this Heaven-ordained and bold Apostle speak of his perils among his own countrymen,[7] for how could he forget, among all his trials, the result of that futile expedient which he adopted in Jerusalem at the suggestion of James, to escape the fury of the "many thousands" of believing Jews, who were "all zealous of the law?"[8] They had heard that he taught the Jews who were among the Gentiles, *to*

[6] Gal. ii. [7] 2 Cor. xi., 26. [8] Acts xxi., 20, 21.

forsake Moses, and not to circumcise their children, nor to walk after the customs. It is therefore proposed that he shall join four brethren who have a vow of the Nazarite,[9] that they may shave their heads, and "that all men," says James, "may know that those things whereof they are informed of thee are nothing; but that *thou thyself walkest orderly, and keepest the law.*" But "those things" were *not* "nothing," for he understood (perhaps not as well then as subsequently) that Christ had fulfilled the law, and that its observance either implied that He had not come, or that, in coming, He had not done what He claimed. Surely Paul meant nothing less than this when he said in his rebuke to Peter, "For if I build again the things which I destroyed (alluding probably to Peter's previous violations of the law in keeping company with Gentiles, and to his knowledge of his freedom in Christ), I am a transgressor;"[10] or in that vehement declaration, "Behold I Paul say unto you, that, if ye be circumcised, Christ shall profit you nothing;"[11] and especially in view of the two verses that follow, for they apply both to Gentile and Jew.

We have thus seen that the Jewish and Judaizing element was so strong in the church at Jerusa-

[9] Acts xxi., 23, 24; Numb. vi., 2-21. [10] Gal. ii., 18; [11] v. 2.

lem, that they held it necessary to circumcise their children, and took pains that the Jews of other churches, even far away, should not depart from Moses, and even tried to bring the Gentiles (apparently with the sanction of James) under the yoke of the ceremonial law. How general, persistent, and successful were the efforts of the Judaizers may be inferred from Paul's frequent and earnest warnings against them. How terribly *cutting* is that name which he gives their formalism, and them, when he says to the Philipians, " Beware of dogs, beware of evil workers, beware of the CONCISION "—this mere amputation, this surgery. [12]

It was because Peter, and James, and John, did not pour the light which they had received themselves, into the Jerusalem church, and because they walked as if they had been in darkness, or twilight, as to Christian liberty, that Paul condemned them as he did. But especially Peter, for he had seen a vision direct from heaven, and then, in confirmation of it, the Holy Ghost given to the uncircumcised when they believed. But the others had both heard and accepted the lesson from him,[13] and were to be blamed for not enforcing it.

Now what shall we say to this apostolic example,

[12] Phil. iii., 2. [13] Acts xi., 1-18.

or to the church at Jerusalem, as a pattern to be copied by Christians in detail, to the letter, and always ? Does our brother, the Jew, who receives and preaches Jesus as the Christ, do wrong in not circumcising his children ? Or does he do the more honor to his Master in loving, trusting, and following Him as "the end of the law for righteousness to every one that believeth ?"[14] But in so acting, neither he, nor any of the Jewish converts, follows James, and the church at Jerusalem, but rather, although not precisely, Paul, and the church at Antioch, where believers on Christ were first called Christians.

Literalists pick what they please from the Scriptures, and try to reproduce it exactly—some one thing, and others another—but much is rejected, or explained away, which, *on their grounds*, ought to be followed ; such as anointing with oil,[15] eating a meal in connection with the communion,[16] washing each others feet,[17] holding property in common,[18] distributing daily to the poor from the common stock,[19] appointing an order of distributors, (deacons ?) who also, like Stephen and Philip, are

[14] Rom. x., 4. [15] Mark vi., 13 ; James v., 14. [16] Matt. xxvi., 21, 23. [17] John xiii., 14. [18] Acts ii., 44, 45 ; v., 1–11. [19] Acts vi., 1.

preachers,[20] laying on of hands,[21] baptism in the name of the Lord Jesus,[22] and many other acts of the Apostles which scrutiny reveals.

The mere fact that it appears in the Acts of the Apostles that believers partook of the Lord's supper after baptism, by no means proves that every believer should be baptized before he communes, and far less that I am bound to exclude my brother from the communion because he differs from me on what constitutes water baptism. How we can regard apostolic example as an infallible guide to the right decision in a case, which, according to our conviction, did not exist in the apostolic times, needs explanation. The Apostles differed among themselves, and so did the early Christians, but not, as far as we know, on the conditions or subjects of water baptism. But what is the situation at present? The great majority of Christians do not regard dipping as essential to the ordinance; while we, the small minority, do. But we all love Christ, and feel that our life is hid with Him in God. In Him we are one. He is the vine, we are the branches; He is the body, we are the members. To all of us His flesh is meat indeed, and His blood is drink indeed.

[20] Acts vi., 13; viii., 5; [21] viii., 17; xix., 6; Heb. vi., 2. [22] Acts viii., 16; x., 48; xix., 5; Rom. vi., 3; Gal. iii., 27.

We all discern, more or less distinctly, the Lord's body in the Lord's supper. Now the question is, *What would the Apostles have done in similar circumstances? Would they have received one another*, or *excluded one another?* The reply that only dipping is baptism, and that we do not read of any but the dipped communing, is irrelevant, for, if we want to be guided by apostolic example, *we must find an analogous case*—a case of serious difference—and mark the conduct of the parties concerned. Look at Paul. What could be more emphatic than his assertions, or more conclusive than his arguments, that Christ had fulfilled the law, and forever freed believers from bondage to its ceremonies? But who was it that withdrew and separated themselves here? It was the Judaizers, who obeyed only part of the letter, and were inflamed with zeal to bring the Gentiles under it all; and Peter was among them. There were bitter dissensions about days and meats among the Romans, but Paul, ever mindful of the unity of the faith, poured the oil of Christian charity upon the troubled waters: "Now the God of patience and consolation grant you to be like-minded one toward another, according to Christ Jesus; that ye may with one mind and one mouth glorify God, even the Father of our Lord Jesus Christ. *Wherefore receive ye one another as Christ also received us to the glory of God.*"[23] "Hast thou faith?" said the same Apostle. (Dost thou believe that nothing but dipping is baptism, and that baptism is essential to communion?) "*Have it to thyself before God.*"[24] But if thou dost exclude thy brother from the Lord's supper, thou judgest him; thou passest upon his qualifications; and it is of thee, I think, that the Apostle asks, "*Who art thou that judgest another man's servant? To his own master he standeth or falleth. Yea, he shall be holden up, for God is able to make him stand.*"[25] It may well seem to many, that, in the spirit of the thing, apostolic example is in favor of open communion.

Although with all the depth and keenness of his great nature, Paul felt the inappropriateness and danger of adhesion to the Mosaic law on the part of Christians, and opposed it against his brother Apostles and all the Judaizing believers, incurring suspicion, hatred, and persecution, yet we find him circumcising Timothy, whose father was a Greek. But we must not think the less of Paul's sincerity on this account, but the more. He knew the difference between general principles and particular cases. This concession was made "because of the Jews,"[26] not

[23] Rom. xv., 5, 6, 7; [24] xiv., 22; [25] xiv., 4; [26] Acts xvi., 3.

in fear, but in the fearless love which longed for their salvation. He would prevent opposition as far as he could, and win them by degrees. "To the Jews," said he, "I became as a Jew, *that I might gain the Jews.*"[27] Behold this dauntless and eloquent champion of freedom from Moses in Christ, bound with a vow of the Nazarite, and trying to carry it out in the temple, but prevented by the fury of the brethren whose suspicions he thus attempts to allay. And this is the grand Apostle, never grander than now, who on looking at the past, which was full of types and shadows that had concealed the substance from all but a few in so many generations, magnified the Christ as "*blotting out the handwriting of ordinances,*" taking *it* "*out of the way,*" and "NAILING IT TO HIS CROSS."[28] And this is his explanation: "To them that are under the law (I became) as under the law, *that I might gain them that are under the law.*" These words, and those which follow, have an important meaning, for they refer to actions, the seeming inconsistency of which required an apology: "To the weak became I as weak, *that I might gain the weak.* I am made all things to all men, *that I might by all means save some.*"

He who holds that these concessions were in things

[27] 1 Cor. ix., 20–22. [28] Col. ii., 14.

indifferent, as many do, who would make the liberty which we have in Christ as nothing, can neither have studied this Apostle nor the early church. He was influenced by his knowledge that the letter of what was then the Scriptures was greatly in favor of the Judaizing believers, and that conscientiously, like himself before his conversion, they were zealous for the law, which they considered as binding forever. "If once divine," they might convincingly argue, "always divine ; if once obligatory, always obligatory ;" and for its duration they might have appealed to the literal words of Moses who delivered it. And how often would "forever" have flashed in their eyes, and rung in their ears! They had no precept for the abolition of their ritual ; and it was easy to think that in its observance they could worship the Christ who had fulfilled it, as well as they had thus anticipated His advent. It was not by the Book that the Council at Jerusalem freed the Gentiles from the yoke which for ages had galled the Jews, but *by the Holy Ghost*,[29] *whose will was read in His outpouring upon the uncircumcised.*[30] Is not the same Spirit with us ? If not, we are not "the body of Christ," but His corpse, His resurrection is in vain, and His promise is broken. But in the still small voice which sounds from the

[29] Acts xv., 28. [30] Acts xi., 17.

present heaven in the believing heart, He still saith, "Lo I am with you always, even unto the end of the world." "Now the Lord is that Spirit."[31] We need not fear that He will lead us to contradict His inspiration,[32] but we may hope that if we open our hearts to Him, and study His work among us, which is no less real to-day than eighteen hundred years ago, He will enlighten our understanding, and help us to rightly interpret His words which are "spirit and life."[33]

While it is evident that in apostolic times it was the custom and delight of believers to be baptized, and then to commune, it is not so clear that none participated but those who had received Christian baptism; for what does Paul mean when he says to the Romans, "Know ye not that *so many of us* as were baptized *into Jesus Christ* were baptized into His *death?*"[34] Were there some, who, having been baptized previous to the resurrection, had neither been baptized into Jesus Christ, nor into His death?* I think that there were (perhaps this was the case of the Ephesian "disciples"), and I think so, notwithstanding the objection that this makes the Apostle argue from a fact which was not applicable to all the

31 2 Cor. iii., 17. 32 1 Pet. i., 10–12. 33 John vi., 63. 34 Rom. vi., 3. * Appendix (8).

members of the Roman church. But that is just what his words imply, and we know that in arguing for the resurrection from baptism for the dead, he alluded to a practice which was not universal.* In writing to the Galatians he seems to intimate by the same distinction, that some of them, as well as of the Romans, had not received Christian baptism : "Ye are all the children of God *by faith* in Jesus Christ ;" then the additional reason, or sign, which was true probably of by far the most of them : "For *as many of you* as have been baptized *into Christ* have *put on* Christ."[35] These had put on His sonship, and hence they were "children" not only "by faith," but also by a Christian profession. It has been supposed that all who were baptized previous to the resurrection, and attached to Christ afterwards, were rebaptized like the Ephesian disciples ; but of this there is no hint, while there is an intimation, as has been shown, to the contrary. It should be noticed that the rebaptisms which are recorded were not administered because the recipients were unfit for communion (Paul styles them "disciples"), but because there had been no recognition of the Holy Ghost at their baptism.†

Ridicule, as we may in others, the habit of follow-

[35] Gal. iii., 26, 27. * Appendix (5). † Appendix (4).

ing the beaten path—treading unthinkingly where their ancestors and friends have trod before them—many of us walk in the same way ourselves. But I am persuaded that on careful study, and reconsideration, there will be a wonderful falling off from the million and more who hold that we are taught by "apostolic example" (1) that water-baptism is absolutely essential to communion; and (2) that, in addition to following our own understanding of the Scriptures, we are bound to exclude our fellow Christians, who cannot see that nothing but dipping is baptism, from the Lord's table.

Regarding both of these inferences as overdrawn, and the second as unscriptural in itself, it seems really terrible for us to demand that they shall be strictly obeyed as if they were the very voice of God; *albeit the Lord Himself established the communion before He even so much as mentioned water baptism with believing.* We ignore the most significant fact that *His death and resurrection came between the last supper and the first apostolical commission to baptize.* Is it Christ, or baptism, that we worship when we insist that His teachings and example shall be set aside for questionable inferences from the action of fallible men, whom their inspired biographer shows to have been neither perfect in their obedience, nor their understanding?

Some of our Baptist papers, which are apt to be mere ledgers of denominational business, varied a little with editorial platitudes, and memoranda of sectarian hopes and fears, spites and likings, ignorance and presumption, are printing arguments for our exclusiveness, which are unworthy of even the straitest of us all. When it is said that the consistent life of the Baptist denomination depends upon close communion, the only possible answer is, that the Baptist denomination ought to die.* If this alleged dependence were as true as some of us believe it false, we ought to mean ourselves every time that we mention "cumberers of the ground." Could the soul-liberty for which Roger Williams went into exile, have gained anything of either strength or consistency from close communion? Was not God on its side, and was not that enough? Witness the Republic to-day, and the fleeing shadow of Union with the State which has darkened the church so long. Must we separate ourselves from our kindred in Christ at His table, to hold consistently that our children should be free to choose their spiritual homes? Must we withdraw from our brethren at

* Appendix (6).

our holiest trysting, before we can be consistent in receiving and administering water baptism as we believe that Christ appointed it ? If we grant that nothing but dipping is baptism, then there is but one belief, the consistent holding of which seems to depend on close communion ; viz., that water baptism, by divine command, should invariably precede the supper. This, however, is the question at issue. But even granting this prerequisite, we must dispose of this other question, "Am I responsible for the observance of this essential by anybody but myself ? "

It is sometimes urged that we protest against pedobaptism and sprinkling by close communion. But to do this by deliberate intent *is to invest the Lord's supper with a foreign and schismatical meaning.* Who are we that we should make His body, which is broken for us, and His blood, which is shed for many, a protest at all, except against our sins ? But to do this in the face of the divine tenderness, the infinite spirituality, and the universal application, of His instituting words, and avowedly *to keep the denomination together*, is both to be guilty of sacrilege, and to glory in our shame.

I am not making a plea for the Lord's supper in opposition, or in preference, to Christian baptism, but a protest against destroying or impairing the divine idea of communion, for mere denominational reasons, or for any whatsoever. It is not fair to represent the open communionists as making much of the Lord's supper and little of baptism; for, as we have seen, the real question at issue, *involves relation and dependence, not comparison;* and therefore we should not consider whether the communion is more sacred, and of higher obligation, than baptism, but whether Christ, who instituted them both, so connected the supper with Christian baptism, that none can partake of the former who have not received the latter; and whether we have anything more to do with the supposed outward qualification than to make it our own. If Christ's teaching and apostolic example clashed, as did Peter's conduct and Paul's, we would be bound to put the servant aside, and follow the Master. But this is not the case with regard to communion. Christ not only gave no hint of water baptism as any sort of a qualification for His supper, but handed the elements to the twelve, who, in the nature of the case, had not received Christian baptism; and we have, as is conceded, no positive precept on the subject from the Apostles. To hold that communion naturally follows baptism is one thing, and to separate ourselves from fellow-members in the body of Christ at His table, who believe in the same order, but differ from us about the form of baptism, is another, and a *non sequitur*.

I think that I have shown that apostolic example neither leads us to this division, nor establishes communion after baptism as the necessary, the invariable, and the God-given order.

WATER BAPTISM AND SPIRIT BAPTISM DISTINGUISHED.

As the form of water baptism has been discussed for centuries in conversations, sermons, and volumes, which in bulk would make millions of Gospels, it cannot but be that the subject seems of far greater importance to many minds than it really is. This result appears inevitable, when we consider how hard it has always been to keep from losing the substance in the form, and to grasp the substance through the form. The over-estimation of water baptism shows itself in the application of many passages of the Scriptures to the washing of the ordinance, instead of the washing of the Spirit, which is an independent action. Hence, as an effect of this misapplication of Scripture, and of this misconnection of the outward with the inward, we have the doctrine of baptismal regeneration, and, I think, in part, at least, the practice of close communion.

Without entering into the question of its nature, its design, and its disappearance, I propose to show that "the gift of the Holy Ghost" was neither dependent upon water baptism, nor invariably connected with it. We have noticed already that the Baptist, in proof of the infinite superiority of his Successor, declared that He would baptize with the Holy Ghost. Christ's prerogative was not in addition to John's, as he stated it, but *in contrast;* for he did not say, "He shall baptize you with water *and* the Holy Ghost," but "*I* indeed have baptized you with *water*, but *He* shall baptize you with the *Holy Ghost.*"[1]

On the last, the great day of the feast, after the libation, which typified the effusion of the Spirit in the times of the Messiah, had been poured from the golden vessel by the priest, who had ascended the altar, Jesus stood and cried, "*He that believeth on me*, as the Scripture has said, out of his belly shall flow rivers of living water."[2] The Evangelist adds, in explanation, that "this spake He of the Spirit *which they that believed on Him* should receive." In that supplementary passage, which closes Mark's Gospel, we find that after saying "He that believeth, *and is baptized*, shall be saved," Jesus added, "These signs shall follow *them that believe;* in my name shall they cast out devils ; *they shall speak with new tongues;* they shall take up serpents ; and if

[1] Mark i., 8. [2] John vii., 38, 39.

they drink any deadly thing it shall not hurt them; and they shall lay hands on the sick and they shall recover." No water baptism is recorded of any of those who saw the vision of cloven tongues, which looked like fire, and who spoke in strange languages "as the Spirit gave them utterance;"[3] and, as we have learned, they could not possibly have received Christian baptism. Under the preaching of Philip, the Samaritans believed, and were baptized, but did not receive the Holy Ghost till Peter and John, who went to them from Jerusalem, prayed for them, and laid their hands upon them.[4] Of course the theologians, who have made up their minds that this miraculous endowment was intimately connected with water baptism, try hard to show that there was something peculiar in this case, which necessitated an exceptional order; but scarcely, I think, with as much success as effort, or ingenuity. It is curious to see how extremes meet in the common belief that this spiritual power was inseparably connected with an outward sign and medium; for here we find Luther and Calvin standing with the Papists, the Anglicans, and some who call themselves Baptists. Luke's history of the Apostles is not a record of rules, but of general development, and of individual,

[3]Acts ii., 3, 4. [4]Acts viii., 12–17.

and often independent, actions. Far be it from me to deny that they are divinely recorded for our spiritual instruction, but not, I believe, in the literal, servile way in which some of us use them. As Peter was preaching in the house of Cornelius, "*the Holy Ghost fell on all them which heard the word;* and they of the circumcision which believed were astonished, because that on the Gentiles also was poured out the gift of the Holy Ghost."[5] These believing Jews thought that circumcision, as a heaven-appointed sign, and condition, of connection with their nation and their religion, was thus connected with the greater blessings of Messiah's reign. Considering the past of this peculiar people, that solitariness of glory which crowned them in their worship of the one and only God in the midst of an idolatrous world, it was neither so strange, not so narrow, for them to think as they did, as for Christians in these days to insist that God's influence on the soul of man, is either invariably or exclusively exercised through certain outward signs. It is not the Lord who has taught us that the Spirit flows either always, or only, in such channels, or is so easily traced, as this; for it was He that said to Nicodemus by night, "The wind bloweth where it listeth (God moves as

[5]Acts x., 44-46.

He pleases), *and thou hearest the sound thereof, but canst not tell whence it cometh, nor whither it goeth. So is every one that is born of the Spirit.*"[6] This utterance, and the other, that "these signs shall follow them that believe," were confirmed when the Holy Ghost fell on those Gentiles, who had neither been circumcised with the knife, not baptized in water, *as He fell on the Apostles at the beginning.*[7] Thus we see that water baptism was not a condition of receiving the gift of the Holy Ghost. Nor when it followed the imposition of hands, as was sometimes the case, were the hands always apostolical, as some, who are anxious for a show of Succession, have labored to prove; for Ananias, who was neither an Apostle, nor, like Philip, one of the seven, *put his hands* on the converted persecutor, and said to him, "Brother Saul, the Lord, even Jesus, that appeared unto thee in the way as thou camest, *hath sent me, that thou mightest receive thy sight, and be filled with the Holy Ghost.*"[8] The context leaves it doubtful, and it is nowhere stated in his writings, whether it was then, when "there fell from his eyes as it had been scales," and previous to his baptism, or afterwards, that Paul began to speak with tongues; but he did tell the Corinthians that he spoke with

[6]John iii., 8. [7]Act xi., 15. [8]Acts ix., 17.

tongues more than they all.[9] It was neither in connection with water baptism, nor with the imposition of hands, that in that overwhelming influence from heaven the gift of tongues was conferred upon the disciples, including the Apostles, who were all with one accord in one place on the day of Pentecost; and the same independence of any accompanying symbol, or visible channel, stands out in the clearest possible light in the case of Cornelius, his kinsmen, and friends. It seems to me that a careful, candid examination of all the communications of the Spirit, miraculously attested, must end in the firm conviction that *they had no outward medium whatever, which was sole and indispensable.*

I now propose to show that water baptism, and Spirit baptism, without these signs, as with them, are clearly distinguished from each other, and are represented as independent of each other, in the word of God.

How often it is when a great spiritual fact is burning for expression, under an allusion to something outward, that *this*, which is merely incidental and far less than secondary, makes more impression, awakens more thought, and incites to more effort, than *that* which has kindled and fed the inward fire!

[9] 1 Cor. xiv., 18.

But as it has been, it is to be feared it will always be, that the outward and temporal will be exalted at the expense of the inward and eternal. The Corinthians baptized the living for the dead, as if the departed were not safe with God, and so did they glory in men, that that most spiritual Apostle, who had heard in the third heaven what it was unlawful to utter, was forced into this scathing rebuke of their idolatry: "I thank God that I baptized none of you, * * * lest any should say that I had baptized in my own name."[10] And so in our day there are many who defend their existence as a denomination on the ground that they are correcting an error in form, or protesting against it, forgetful surely how grateful Paul was for infinitely better work when he declared that Christ had sent him *not to baptize*, BUT TO PREACH THE GOSPEL.[11]

Believing the good news of redeeming love involved, and still involves, the baptism of the Spirit. In applying Christianity to social life, husbands are exhorted by Paul to love their wives, even as Christ also loved the church, and gave Himself for it, that He might sanctify and cleanse it with *the washing of water* (or, literally, in the font of water) BY, OR IN, THE WORD.[12] There is doubtless an allusion to water

[10]Cor. i., 14, 15. [11]Verse 17. [12]Eph. v., 25, 26.

baptism, but who can say that the font of water does not stand for Him who holds the sanctifying and cleansing power? "Sanctify them through Thy truth," was Christ's prayer for His people,—"Thy word is truth."[13] John called *Him* the Word, and He promised to send the Comforter; "for," said He, "if I depart, I will send Him unto you;" and again, "He shall glorify me, *for He shall receive of mine,* and shall show it unto you. *All things that the Father hath are mine;* therefore said I that He shall take of mine, and shall show it unto you."[14] "Thus," says Alford,—although a believer in baptismal regeneration,—"*the word* preached and received, is the conditional element of purification—*the real water of spiritual baptism;* that wherein and whereby alone the efficacy of baptism is conveyed; that wherein and whereby we are regenerated, the process of sanctification being subsequent and gradual."

So must we understand the Apostle, when, in showing the nature of salvation to Titus, he writes, "Not by works of righteousness which we have done, but according to His mercy He saved us, by the washing (*διὰ λουτροῦ,* by the font) of regeneration, and renewing of the Holy Ghost, which He shed on

[13] John xvii., 17. [14] John xvi., 7, 14, 15.

us abundantly *through Jesus Christ, our Saviour.*"[15] To the same effect is Paul's contrast of the present with the past of the Corinthians: "And such were some of you; but ye are *washed*, but ye are sanctified, but ye are justified in the name of the Lord Jesus, and by (*in*) *the Spirit of our God.*"[16]

If we consider the case of a believer who has not been buried in water, and raised out of it, but who has been separated from sin as his tyrant, and lifted into newness of life, I think we shall see that he is "buried with Christ in baptism, wherein also he is risen with Him, *through the faith of the operation of God*, who hath raised Him from the dead."[17]

The Pedobaptist believer, or rather his parents, may have mistaken both the subject and mode of water baptism, and yet be none the less baptized in the Spirit, and hence really, because divinely and eternally, baptized. The baptism "unto Moses in the cloud and in the sea" is fulfilled in our baptism into one body by one Spirit unto Christ, who leads us through the real wilderness to the real Canaan; and, like the Israelites, we all eat the same spiritual meat, and drink the same spiritual drink, for we drink of that spiritual Rock that follows us, and that Rock is Christ.[18]

[15] Titus iii., 5, 6. [16] 1 Cor. vi., 11. [17] Col. ii., 12, Rom. vi., 4. [18] 1 Cor. x., 2, 3, 4.

It was an inspired teacher who taught that the outward sign might exist without the inward grace, and also that the inward grace gave the only good title to the name which was claimed on account of the outward sign: "For he is *not* a Jew which is one *outwardly*, neither is that circumcision which is outward in the flesh; but he *is* a Jew which is one inwardly, and circumcision is that *of the heart*, *in the spirit*, and *not* in the letter, whose praise is not of men, but of God."[19]

Paul applied this principle to the Philipians when he wrote to them thus, although many of them were uncircumcised "in the letter:" "For *we are the circumcision which worship God in the spirit, and rejoice in Christ Jesus, and have no confidence in the flesh.*"[20] To the Colossians also his words were no less dubious: "Ye are complete in Him, which is the Head of all principality and power; *in whom also ye are circumcised with the circumcision made without hands in putting off the body of the sins of the flesh by the circumcision of Christ.*"[21] When he wished to show the Fountain of that union which makes believers "one body in Christ, and every one members one of another,"[22] he represented the Spirit

19 Rom. ii., 28, 29. 20 Phil. iii., 3. 21 Col. ii., 10, 11. 22 Rom. xii., 5.

as the element in which Christians were buried; "for," said he, "in one Spirit (ἐν ἑνὶ πνεύματι) were we all baptized (ἐβαπτίσθημεν) into one body, * * * and were all made to drink (ἐποτίσθημεν) one spirit."[23] How complete the statement! He is describing a spiritual operation by a figure which takes the subject into the element, but for fear that this may seem merely external, he adds a second, which takes the element into the subject. Any allusion to the cup in the Lord's supper is obviated by the tense of the verb to drink, and also by the fact that it is not the Holy Ghost, but the blood of Christ, that is represented by the wine of the communion. Then, again, the observance of the Lord's supper by the same persons is frequent, because it represents, and is, when properly observed, *a habitual process*—living spiritually on Christ—but water baptism *symbolizes something already done, and is not to be repeated.* This is a real distinction, and should not be overlooked in treating of the two ordinances.

Showing how clearly Spirit baptism was distinguished from water baptism, and how the latter in value and importance was not to be named beside the former, neither Luke, nor John, who was certainly the most spiritual of the four, mentions it as

[23] 1 Cor. xii., 13.

enjoined by the Saviour in the apostolical commission, which was delivered after the resurrection (and in which alone He ever enjoined it) ; but both make ample records of the promise of the inestimable blessing which the ordinance symbolizes. It must be known to many of my readers that the last eleven verses of Mark's Gospel are regarded by many of the ablest and devoutest of orthodox Biblical scholars as an addition from another and a later hand. If this be so, then of the four evangelists Matthew alone presents water baptism as a commandment of Christ ; but it does not appear that the formula given in this Gospel was adopted by the Apostles, or their contemporaries. I do not state these facts to weaken the obligation of water baptism, but merely to shed light from the Scriptures on its relative importance.

It appears that the Corinthians craved the gift of tongues as a sign of superior spiritual power, but Paul, who was pre-eminent in this miraculous endowment, told them that he would rather speak five words in the church with his understanding, that by his voice he might teach others also, than ten thousand words in an unknown tongue.[24] He had instructed them that no man could say that Jesus was the Lord but by the Holy Ghost, and that though

[24] 1 Cor. xiv., 19.

there were diversities of gifts, there was but one Spirit.[25] Then, in revelation of the "more excellent way," he rises suddenly and swiftly, like a lark to the rising sun, into that eulogy of love, in which we seem to hear the very music of heaven. More emphatic, if not so melodious and so moving, is John's teachings of the same truth: "Beloved, let us love one another; *for love is of God, and every one that loveth is born of God.* * * * * *God is love.* If we love one another, *God dwelleth in us,* and His love is perfected in us. *Hereby* know we that we *dwell in Him, and He in us,* because He hath given us of His Spirit."[26] It is then in the divine love that we are baptized into one body, and it is this which is the water of life, of which we drink, and live forever.

[25] 1 Cor. xii., 3, 4. [26] 1 John iv., 7, 8, 12, 13.

INTERCOMMUNION.

The history of the past, and our knowledge of the human mind, forbid us to cherish the hope that there will ever be uniformity of belief and practice among Christians. They have differed, they do differ, and they will differ, on many matters of organization, ordinance, and doctrine. Some of us think, that, all things considered, it is better so; that truth being many-sided, and not fully seen by any one pair of eyes, it is well that special prominence is given to this feature by some, and to that by others. Even where we think we find grave errors, we may discover by further search, if our hearts are right, that some phase of truth, overlooked, or more than half concealed elsewhere, is there brought out into bold relief. And so a grander revelation, and a more potential influence, are secured for truth in the world.

He is to be pitied who believes that it is only his sect which has a Christian mission to fulfil, and therefore a right to live; for he must feel that the Redeemer's kingdom is in a sad plight; yes, and hopeless, unless he is so young or so foolish as to fancy that he can either reason, coax, or terrify mankind into his way of thinking. Whether the Pope believes that this is possible, or simply that it is his duty to persist in the attempt, he has recently given another illustration of this doubtless pious folly. Like a great many Protestants, of whom he should logically be the "one pastor," he confounds Christian union with ecclesiastical unity—two things which are entirely distinct, and which indeed could scarcely exist together. "The church is one," says the Pope. Granted. "But what one is it?" he continues, "for the self-styled churches are many." "It is the Holy Catholic church," he replies, meaning, of course, his own, while the hierarchy, and the millions whom it guides, respond, "It is, and amen." It is the Baptist church, cries a Baptist, and is sustained by quite a general response from his brethren. It is the Episcopal church, says the High Churchman (*sotto voce*, we, and the Catholics), casting a look of filial longing on the grand proportions of the holy mother of Rome. Now, who is to decide between these three claimants and all the others, who cla'm, at least, to be churches of Christ? The Bible? No; for it is on this that they disagree. It has no voice of its own except to the individual soul. If he speaks for it, its voice is lost, or rather blended, in his. Its meaning may be in his words, and it may not; and it is likely to lose volume, or take coloring, in passing through the medium. He is interpreter, and it, in its silence, still lies open for interpretation. What follows? Either the Catholic church, in the papal sense, as an infallible interpreter, with ecclesiastical unity; or the exercise of private interpretation, with honest, earnest, outspoken, and manifold differences. He knows little of God's truth, and does not dream how much of it we have yet to learn, who fears this ordeal on its account; and he ought to hide himself, and be at rest, in the church of Rome. Every interpretation should stand on its own merits; and nothing should be rejected simply because it is "heterodox"—the other, the contrary, the minority opinion. All we who are brethren should recognize, respect, and hear, the teachers who are raised up among us by our One Master, but we should examine their teaching, each for himself. "Quench not the Spirit, despise not prophesying; prove all things, hold fast that which is good."[1] This was no more the duty and the privilege of the Thessalonians than it is ours, who have now a more complete and accessible standard, as well as the light which shines from eighteen centu-

[1] 1 Thess. v., 19–21.

ries of developing Christianity, and the help of the ever-present Christ if we but desire it.

Christendom will neither be Roman Catholic, Episcopal, nor Baptist. Differences will increase with thought and intelligence, but so will Christian union. In the changing of opinions, differences are multiplying now, but there never was a time when the search for the source of Christian union was more ardent, or the consciousness of it deeper, and more general. How do the old school and the new school agree? Not in the doctrine of the atonement, for so much is involved in this single question, that, if the Christian heart did not enter in at once as a criterion and a harmonizer, we might think that the two parties worshipped two different Gods. Their real union does not lie in their consolidation; for if they agree to differ, their consolidation means simply mutual toleration; and if they still differ and contend, their consolidation is but an ill-fitting cloak for their disagreement to wear. How then are the old and the new school one? In loving the living Christ, and in living by the loving Christ. Thus, thus only, and thus always, they are one. They may have different creeds, or conflicting interpretations of the same creed, they may have different colleges, and they may have different churches, but still in loving the living Christ, and in living by the loving Christ, they have the same spirit, and the same life, they are of the same family, and they have the same Father, and the Heavenly Jerusalem is the home and the mother of them all. Thus for Christians, notwithstanding their differences—for the Catholic and the Quaker, the Baptist and the Anglican, for Doctor Bushnell and for Doctor Hodge, for you and for me, the prayer of Jesus for us all has its answer from God: "That they all may be one; as Thou, Father, art in Me, and I in Thee, that they also may be one in us." It has never been unanswered since it was offered, for under the noise and confusion of scholastic and sectarian strife, heaven has always been conscious of the deep dumb music of love to God in the Christian's heart, and to "his brother also."[2] Sweeter to the risen Christ than the hallelujahs of the seraphim has been this responsive throb to His own heart in the heart of His bride, His mystical body, His indivisible church.

But has He left us no sign, and no visible means, of this union to each other, and to Him? Why did He institute the communion before He built His church on Peter, and before he revived to be Himself its Chief Corner-stone? Why do we read the

[2] 1 John iv., 21.

sacred story of the last supper before the account of the first Christian church? Because, it seems to me, the Lord intended to keep the communion as His memorial, as the special sign and a potent means of our life by Him, and of our union with each other, free from all ecclesiastical and doctrinal differences—differences which began with the Apostles and the church at Jerusalem, and continue to this day, with no prospect of reconcilement—except in Christian liberty and in Christian love.

Suppose that the Lord, foreseeing the development of His kingdom as it has developed, and is developing, had instituted an ordinance to portray Himself as the source of life, and His disciples as united to each other in Him, what more appropriate formula could He employ than that which we repeat from His lips so often at His table? There is no hint of indorsing difference, for no difference is hinted, and no suggestion that previous water baptism is required, for water baptism as a Christian rite had not been commanded; but simply, of the bread, "This is my body which is broken for you: this do in remembrance of Me;" and of the wine, "This cup is the new testament in my blood: this do, as oft as ye drink it, in remembrance of Me."[3] There is nothing

[3] 1 Cor. xi., 23–26.

here to make the Baptist missionary separate himself in the presence of both converted and unbelieving heathen from his brethren in the Christian ministry, who have left home in the same spirit, and are spending themselves for the same Saviour, and the same souls. Why then should this scandal remain? How contradictory it must seem to idolaters that though their strange teachers believe in one Saviour, by whose death they are reconciled to God, and by whose life they are saved from sin, they yet refuse to partake of His body, which was broken for them, and of His blood, which was shed for their pardon, together! "Can each believe that the same Christ died for the other, and that they all are united in living by Him?" is the almost inevitable inquiry which it is hard to answer to the satisfaction of the inquirer. And if we had as good eyes as the heathen, would it not seem most strange and sad that members of churches whose ministers exchange, who mingle together in meetings for prayer, who are heart to heart and shoulder to shoulder in the Master's work, separate from each other at His table, even when Providence has gathered them around it together? What word is there in the Bible which makes it our duty to prevent Christian parents (as our *invitation* prevents them) from showing forth in our churches, with their children, born again in Christ, "His death until He come?" And yet we compel the Christian father to go away, or remain as an alien spectator, while his believing child partakes, may be, for the *first* time of the communion. How repugnant to the thought of their union in nature, their union in grace, and their union in glory! A triple schism seems more than lurking in this awful division. Verily, we ought to have a "thus saith the Lord" for such a separation as this; but it never was uttered, and it cannot be found.

It is vain to put the observance of the first day of the week, and the exclusion of fellow-members in Christ from the communion, on the same ground; for, in the absence of positive precepts, and considering the cases on their own merits, we see propriety beautifying the one, and something worse than impropriety distorting the other. If Christ died and rose again from the dead as the Saviour of the world, should not the world commemorate His resurrection? Does not nature demand a rest at stated intervals, and a chance to meditate? Should she ever forget her Redeemer, or thrust her hand into the old dispensation for the Jewish Sabbath, as if the creation of the world were so glorious as the new birth of the soul? "Let no man therefore judge you in meat or in drink, or in respect of a holiday, or of the new moon, or of the Sabbath days, *which are a shadow of things to come.*"[4] What we call Sunday, John called the *Lord's* day, and it was was held sacred to Christian services by the earliest Christians. But as there is no commandment concerning it, and as all our time, with all our heart, belongs to Christ, there is liberty in its observance. "One man esteemeth one day above another: *another esteemeth every day alike. Let every man be fully persuaded in his own mind.*" Thus the observance of the Lord's day is left with the individual Christian, and safely too, though some are afraid. It is safe to do a good thing without a commandment, especially when you have an example, but what is it, without either, to do something which of itself more than suggests that Christians are not "one bread and one body," which, in connection with this very ordinance, they are most solemnly declared to be? Paul teaches that this union is implied and effected by communing together. What then is the implication and effect of exclusion?

Let churches of different names celebrate the communion together, not as a pretence that they do not differ in many respects, but to illustrate and cherish

[4] Col. ii., 14–17.

their common life in Christ, and their fellowship with each other. We often worship together, and feel that the house of each is our Father's also ; we meet in mingled sorrow, love, and hope, around the sainted dead ; let us mingle in communion. God is one Father, Christ is one Saviour, Christians are one family, Heaven is one home ; let us sit together under His cross by the way. So sat the twelve all unwittingly on the night of His betrayal ; but to us, now, the empty sepulchre and the angels appear with Calvary, and our gathering is radiant with the tenderest of Heaven's glory in the smile of the Christ who is risen.

APPENDIX.

(1.)

"For he that eateth and drinketh unworthily, eateth and drinketh damnation to himself, not discerning the Lord's body" (1 Cor. xi., 29).

Alford says of this often quoted text, which is so generally and so horribly misunderstood, because the context is not sufficiently considered: "Eats and drinks JUDGMENT to himself; *i. e.*, brings on himself judgment by eating and drinking. *κρῖμα*, as is evident by verses 30–32 is not 'damnation,' (*κατάκριμα*) as rendered in our English version, a mistranslation which has done infinite mischief."

That this point is well taken, is clear from the verses cited, for we find in them that they who had incurred *κρῖμα* were not "damned," but weak, sickly, and asleep, which adjectives some commentators understand in a spiritual sense, and others in the literal, the latter seeing an allusion to a prevailing epidemic; also, that if these Corinthians had judged themselves, they would not have been judged ; and, finally, that when they were judged, they were chastened of the Lord, "*that they should not he condemned with the world.*"

"*Not discerning the Lord's body,*" explains their case. Connected as the Lord's supper was, at its institution, with the passover, the Corinthians made it an occasion of indecent excess. One was "hungry," and another was "drunken." They therefore lost the spiritual significance and benefit of the celebration ; and disregarding and changing its sacred character, they were "guilty of the body and blood of the Lord." Not so with the penitent, no matter how heinous his sins, who takes Christ as his Saviour, and thus humbly and trustfully, or even timidly, communes. It was for such that Jesus came, and it is for such that His table is spread.

(2.)

"They devoted themselves to the careful study of the text, and laid down rules for transcribing it with the most scrupulous precision.

"A saying is ascribed to Simon the Just (B. C. 300–290), the last of the succession of the men of the Great Synagogue, which embodies the principle on which they acted, and enables us to trace the growth of their system. 'Our fathers have taught us,' he said, 'three things': 'to be cautious in judging, to train many scholars, and to set a fence about the law.' They wished to make the law of Moses the rule of life for the whole nation, and for individual men. But it lies in the nature of every such law, of every informal, half-systematic code, that it raises questions which it does not solve. The Jewish teacher could recognize no principles beyond the precepts of the law. The result showed that in this as in other instances *the idolatry of the letter was destructive of the very reverence in which it had originated.* Decisions on fresh questions were accumulated into a complex system of casuistry. The 'Words of the Scribes' now used as a technical phrase for these decisions, were honored above the law. It was a greater crime to offend against them than the law. They were as wine while the precepts of the law were as water. The first step was taken toward annulling the commandments of God for the sake of their own traditions. The casuistry became at once subtle and prurient, evading the plainest duties, tampering with conscience (Matt. xv., 1–6; xxiii., 16–23). The right relation of moral and ceremonial laws was not only forgotten, but absolutely inverted. *This was the result of the profound reve-*

rence for the letter which gave no heed to the Word abiding in them.—John v., 38 (Dr. Wm. Smith's New Testament History).

(3.)

The Proselytes of Righteousness, known also as Proselytes of the Covenant, were perfect Israelites. We learn from the Talmud, that, in addition to circumcision, baptism was also required to complete their admission to the faith. The proselyte was placed in a tank, or pool, up to his neck in water. His teachers, who now acted as his sponsors, repeated the great commandments of the law. These he promised and vowed to keep, and then, with an accompanying benediction, he plunged under the water. To leave one hand-breadth of his body unsubmerged would have vitiated the whole rite (Ugolini, 22). The Rabbis carried back the origin of the baptism to a remote antiquity, finding it in the command of Jacob (Gen. xxxv., 2), and of Moses (Ex. xix., 10). The Targum of the Pseudo-Jonathan inserts the word "Thou shalt circumcise and *baptize*" in Ex. xii., 44. Even in the Ethiopic version of Matt. xxiii., 15, we find "compass sea and land to *baptize* one proselyte." The baptism was followed, as long as the temple stood, by the offering or Corban (Dr. Wm. Smith's New Testament History).

Perhaps there was an allusion to these unrequired baptisms in the question which Christ put to the pharisees: "The baptism of John, was it from Heaven (as he claimed) or (like your baptism of proselytes) of men?"

When *men* were admitted as proselytes, three rites were performed—*circumcision*, *baptism*, and *oblation*; when *women*, two—*baptism* and *oblation*. The baptism was administered in the day-time, by immersion of the whole person; and while standing in the water, the proselyte was instructed in certain portions of the law. The whole families of proselytes, including infants, were baptized. It is most probable that John's baptism in outward form resembled that of proselytes. Some (De Wette, Winer, Paulus, Meyer) deny that the proselyte baptism was in use before the time of John; but *the contrary has been generally supposed and maintained* (cf. Lightfoot, Schöttgen, Buxtorf, Wetstein, Bengel). *Indeed the baptism or lustration of a proselyte would follow as a matter of course by analogy from the constant legal practice of lustration after all uncleanesses; and it is difficult to imagine a time when it would not be in use.* Besides it is highly improbable that the Jews should have borrowed the rite from the Christians, or the Jewish hierarchy from John (Alford's Greek Test., Matt. iii. 6).

The following passage shows that the baptism of John did not seem like an innovation to Josephus, who was contemporaneous with the Apostles, and thoroughly versed in the laws and customs of the Jews. His account of Herod's reasons for killing the Baptist does not conflict with those of Matthew and Mark. The historian gives none but political causes, probably because he knew, and could think, of no other, while the Evangelists, who were more interested and better informed in the facts of John's career, are more specific in their statement :

"Now, some of the Jews thought that the destruction of Herod's army (by his father-in-law, Aretas, who made war upon him on account of his desertion of his wife, and his adultery with Herodias) came from God, and that very justly, as a punishment for what he did against John, that was called the *Baptist;* for Herod slew him, who was a good man, and commanded the Jews to exercise virtue, both as to righteousness toward one another, and piety towards God, and so to come to baptism ; for that the washing would be acceptable to Him, if they made use of it not in order to the putting away of some sins, but for the purification of the body : supposing still that the soul was thoroughly purified beforehand by righteousness. Now when others came in crowds about him, for they were greatly moved by hearing his words, Herod, who feared lest the great influence John had over the people might put it into his power and inclination to raise a rebellion (for they seemed ready to do anything he should advise) thought it best, by putting him to death, to prevent any mischief he might cause, and not to bring himself into difficulties by sparing a man who might make him repent of it when it should be too late. Accordingly he was sent a prisoner, out of Herod's suspicious temper, to Macherus, the castle I before mentioned, and was there put to death. Now the Jews had an opinion that the destruction of this army was sent as a punishment upon Herod, and a mark of God's displeasure against him" (Antiquities of the Jews, book xviii., chap. vi., sec. 2).

(4.)

And it came to pass, that while Apollos was at Corinth, Paul having passed through the upper coasts came to Ephesus, and finding certain disciples, he said unto them, Have ye received the Holy Ghost since ye believed? And they said unto him, We have not so much as heard whether there be any Holy Ghost. And he said unto them, Unto what then were ye baptized? And they said, Unto John's baptism. Then said Paul, John verily baptized with the baptism of repentance, saying unto the people, that they should believe on Him which should come after him, that is, Christ Jesus. When they heard this, they were baptized in the name of the Lord Jesus. And when Paul had laid his hands upon them, the Holy Ghost came on them; and they spake with tongues and prophesied. And all the men were about twelve (Acts xix., 1—7).

An attempt, as bold as it is absurd, has been made to reverse the meaning and obviate the consequences of this account, by taking the words, "that is, Christ Jesus," from Paul's mouth, and putting them into John's, and then applying the following verse, "When they heard this, they were baptized in the name of the Lord Jesus," to the multitude that John baptized in Jordan, and therefore to the men that Paul was addressing.

But the passages which I have quoted in the chapter to which this note belongs, show beyond a doubt that the Baptist did not know that Jesus *was the Lord* till after His baptism, and the promised attestation of His Messiahship; and that these took place when the Baptist's work was well nigh (if not entirely) finished.

If John baptized in the name of the Lord Jesus, he was not a prophet in the Old Testament sense, he did not belong to the Legal Dispensation, his baptism was not unto repentance, and he had not, any more than the Apostles, disciples of his own; for they knew Jesus as a man, and by baptism into His natural name, with His Messianic title added, they professed their faith in Him as the historical personal Christ of the Gospels. But these Gospels tell us that this was the very thing that those men questioned, and that they followed another master.

If the Baptist baptized in the name of the Lord Jesus, then "all the people that heard him, and the publicans, being baptized with the baptism of John," ought to have considered themselves, and to have acted, as professed Christians in the presence of the Christ; but they did not seem to know that they were His baptized disciples.

It is confessed that it was for fear of encouraging the "Anabaptists" that Calvin so grossly misinterpreted this unmistakeable rebaptism; and it is to be feared that some of us have followed this illustrious leader with an equally interested, although a different, design; namely, to free the baptism of John from Paul's opinion of its insufficiency, in view of the fact that it, and it only, had been administered to two of the Apostles who partook of the Lord's supper at its institution.

But Alford's interpretation of this re-baptism based on a literal rendering of the tenses puts the act in still a stronger light :

"These seem to have been in the same situation as Apollos. They cannot have been mere disciples of John, on account of πιστεύσαντες, which can bear no meaning but that of believing on the *Lord Jesus* ; but they had received only John's baptism, and had had no proof of the descent of the Holy Spirit, nor knowledge of His gifts.

ἐλαβ. πιστεύς. The aorist should be faithfully rendered, not as in the English Version, '*Have ye received the Holy Ghost since ye believed ?*' but 'DID ye receive the Holy Ghost WHEN YE BECAME BELIEVERS ?' i. e., '*on your becoming believers had ye the gifts of the Spirit conferred on you ?*'—as in ch. viii. 16, 17. This is both grammatically necessary (see also Rom., xiii., 11, εγγύτερον ἡμων ἡ σωτηρία ἡ ὅτε ἐπιστεύσαμεν) and absolutely demanded by the sense ; the enquiry being not as to any reception of the Holy Ghost during the period *since* their baptism, but as to one simultaneous with their first reception into the church:* and their not having then received Him is accounted for by the deficiency of their baptism.†

ἀλλ οὐδε, ON THE CONTRARY, not even * * * *ἠκούσαμεν*. Here again, not, 'we *have not* heard,' but WE DID NOT HEAR at the time of our conversion: —Our reception into the faith was unaccompanied by any preaching of the office or the gifts of the Spirit,—our baptism was not followed by any imparting of His gifts: WE DID NOT SO MUCH AS HEAR HIM MENTIONED. . . . . . .

Two singular perversions of this verse have occurred. 1. The Anabaptists use it to authorize the repetition of Christian baptism;‡ whereas, it is not Christian baptism which was repeated, *seeing that John's baptism was not such*, but only the baptism which they now for the first time received; and, 2. Beza, Calixtus, Calv., Suicer, Glass., Buddeus, Wolf, *et al.*,

*If these "disciples" were members of a Christian church (and why were they not?) it is probable that they had often communed.

†For proofs that the gift of the Spirit did not depend on previous water baptism, see "Water Baptism and Spirit Baptism Distinguished."

‡"Anabaptists" (Baptists, we call ourselves) do not regard the sprinkling of infants as "Christian baptism;" and hence, in intention, to say nothing of fact, no more deserve the nick-name than Paul.

wishing to wrest this weapon out of the hands of the Anabaptists, oddly enough suppose this verse to belong still to Paul's discourse, and to mean, '*and the people when they heard him* (*John*) *were baptised into the name of the Lord Jesus.*' This obviously is contrary to fact historically: and would leave our present narrative in a singular state; for Paul, having treated their baptism as *insufficient* would thus proceed on it to impose his hands as if it were sufficient."

Alford also discusses in this connection the general question of rebaptism. "Was it," says he, "the ordinary practice to re-baptize those who had been baptized either by John or by the disciples *before baptism became, by the effusion of the Holy Spirit*, λουτρὸν παλιγγενεσίας? This we cannot definitely answer. That it was *sometimes* done this incident shows: *but in all probability, in the cases of the majority of the original disciples, the greater baptism by the Holy Ghost and fire on the day of Pentecost superseded the outward form or sign. The Apostles themselves received only this baptism* (besides probabably that of John) *and most likely the same was the case with the original believers.* But of the three thousand who were added on the day of Pentecost, very many must have been already baptized by John, *and all were baptized without inquiry.*"

(5.)

Else what shall they do, who are baptized for the dead, if the dead rise not at all? why are they then baptized for the dead? (1 Cor. xv., 29).

To such an extreme has the doctrine of Indorsement been carried, that the Scriptures are twisted out of their plainest, fairest meanings, for fear that there shall ever seem to be an allusion to a reprehensible practice without an express condemnation of it—as if you must say that you do not like the devil or a mosquito, whenever you mention either. Thus it happens that many commentators have puzzled their brains, and contradicted their scholarship, or revealed their ignorance, to invent explanations of this passage, to show that Paul does not allude to baptism for the dead, because he does not stop in his magnificent argument to expressly condemn that practice.

This common idea should make those who hold it, regard music, dancing, drinking, and other convivialities as divine, for Jesus alluded to them, sometimes in the most sacred and precious connections, without a word of condemnation.

Fortunately, however, for the case in hand, ὑπέρ

for those who know its meaning, is a hard fence to vault, and very important in limiting other passages. Then there is so much honesty and common sense in the following interpretation by Alford, that it needs simply to be read to win its way:

ἐπεί resumes the main argument, which has been interrupted by the explanation, since ver. 23, of *ἕκαστος ἐν τῷ ἰδίῳ τάγματι.* After it is an ellipsis of "if it be as the adversaries suppose."

τί ποιήσουσιν.—There is in these words a tacit reprehension of the practice about to be mentioned, which it is hardly possible altogether to miss. Both by the third person, and by the article before *βαπτ.*, he indirectly separates himself, and those to whom he is writing, from participation in, or approval of the practice:—the meaning being what WILL BECOME OF—what account can they give of their practice?

οἱ βαπτιζόμενοι, THOSE WHO ARE IN THE HABIT OF BEING BAPTIZED—not *οἱ βαπτισθέντες.* The distinction is important as affecting the interpretation. See below.

ὑπὲρ τῶν νεκρῶν, ON behalf of THE DEAD; viz., *the same νεκροί*, who are spoken of in the next clause, and throughout the chapter, as the subjects of *ἀνάστασις*,—not *νεκροί* in any figurative sense. *τῶν νεκρ.*, the article marking the particular dead persons on behalf of whom the act took place.

Before we pass to the exegesis, it will be well to go through the next question—ἐι ὅλως κ.τ.λ. IF DEAD MEN ARE NOT RAISED AT ALL, WHY DO THEY TROUBLE THEMSELVES TO BE BAPTIZED FOR THEM?

Thus much being said as to the plain meaning of the words used, there can be no doubt as to their interpretation. *The only legitimate reference* is to a practice, not otherwise known to us, not mentioned here with any approval by the Apostle, not generally prevalent (οἱ βαπτ.), but in use by some,—of *survivors allowing themselves to be baptized on behalf of* (believing ?) *friends who had died without baptism.* With the subsequent similar practices of the Cerinthians and Marcionites, this may or may not have been connected. All we clearly see from the text, is, *that it unquestionably did exist* (Alford's Greek Test. *in loc.* So also Ambrose and Anselm, Erasmus, Grotius, *al.*, and recently by Billroth, Rückert, Meyer, De Wette, *al.*).

The same author says that the following from Stanley is worth quoting: "On the whole therefore this explanation of the passage (*given above*) may be safely accepted, 1, as exhibiting a curious relic of primitive superstition, which after having, as the words imply (?) prevailed generally in the apostolical church, gradually dwindled away till it was only to be found in some obscure sects where it lost its original significance; 2, as containing an example of the Apostle's mode of dealing with a practice with which he could have no real sympathy; not condemning or ridiculing it, but appealing to it, as an expression, however distorted, of their better feelings."*

(6.)

To show the kind of statements which pass current among us, with the editorial indorsement of such an able and candid journal as the *Watchman and Reflector*, I quote a few of forty-one "Facts on Baptism and Communion," by Rev. J. C. Foster of Beverly, Mass.

"28. *It is a fact* that Baptists are not responsible for the separation of Christians at the Lord's table, since they could not unite there with the unimmersed without the violation of their consciences, *while the unimmersed could unite with them without paying such a price, by being immersed, holding as they do that immersion is baptism,* while Baptists hold that sprinkling is not baptism."

By observing the italics, it will be seen that a

*For other expressions of this interpretation, and for different interpretations see Lange's Commentary.

very important fact is ignored in this assertion; namely, that Pedobaptists believe that *sprinkling* is as valid water-baptism as immersion, and hence, that, *according to their conscience* ANABAPTISM would be the "price" of communing with us on our terms. The *petitio principii* which precedes this evident blunder, is to be found in the assumption, that *the "consciences" of close-communion Baptists are the standards by which their responsibility for the separation of Christians at the Lord's table is to be decided.* Then, again, when Mr. Foster says that "*Baptists* cannot unite," &c., he either implies that such men as Bunyan and Hall, Spurgeon and Noel, are *not* Baptists, or that they and the thousands who agree with them, are not worthy of consideration at all. Which is it—an attempted monopoly of the name, or a want of respect for respectable brethren?

"29. *It is a fact* that all that is necessary for all Christians to be united at the Lord's table, is for all to be baptized according to what all agree is baptism."

Here the blunder of "Fact 28" is repeated; for Pedobaptists, who have been baptized by either one of the two forms which they consider equally valid, cannot submit to immersion, because they feel that in their cases it would be rebaptism. I cannot account for such blundering as this, which would almost prove even a tyro in logic a dunce, except on the supposition that we do not believe that anybody has a conscience on water baptism except ourselves.

"30. *It is a fact* that the advocates of what is called 'open communion' demand of Baptists *that they should solemnly sanction sprinkling as baptism, when they most honestly and decidedly believe that it is not baptism.*"

Who are meant by the advocates of open communion? If its Baptist friends, Mr. Foster should know that most of them advocate it on the ground that the Scriptures do not make water baptism a prerequisite to the Lord's supper; and others, because they believe that on this matter every man should be fully persuaded in his own mind, and that each is responsible for himself, and to the Lord alone. If Mr. Foster means the Pedobaptist advocates of open communion, it is a question whether it is either modest or safe for him to speak for them in such a sweeping and dogmatic style. I never meet Pedobaptists who ask me to believe more than the *sincerity* of their belief that sprinkling is baptism, and that they consider themselves baptized.

31 "*It is a fact* that for Baptists to go to the table of other denominations (not the Lord's?) would require a sacrifice of

conscience, while for other denominations to come to them *would require only the sacrifice of convenience*."

What does this statement mean? It is really an accusation to this effect,—that while "other denominations" profess to regard sprinkling, and immersion, equally valid water baptism, *they really think so of immersion only;* for how otherwise can the question of their immersion, *they having been sprinkled, and regarding sprinkling as valid baptism*, be simply one of "convenience?" This looks as if my supposition that we are sure that we have the monopoly of conscience on water baptism, were too well founded, especially in view of the fact that the editor indorsed the article under criticism, as follows: "It gives in the tersest manner forty or more FACTS that are telling because truthful." They would all be "telling" in the editorial sense, if they were all "truthful;" but those of them which are not truthful, are still exceedingly "telling"—only in another direction.

34. *It is a fact* that the Lord's supper was not instituted for the purpose of manifesting brotherly love, or demonstrating *liberality*, and that its open observance does not enable those who might commune together, if they would, to love each other any better for this questionable privilege."

The latter half of this statement is not a Papal, but

it is a close-communion-Baptist, *bull.* Behold the curious blending of the indicative and the potential !—" its open observance *does not* enable those who *might* commune together, if they *would,* to love each other any better for this *questionable privilege.*" Of course it doesn't; for if Mr. Foster can say of any Christians, they "*might commune together if they would,*" it is to be inferred, if he understands their case, *that they don't.* "*Questionable* privilege," in this connection, is mild phraseology; but, under these conditions, it is hard to find anything more appropriate. Whether a slip of the printer's hand, or of Mr. Foster's pen, it is quite as good as the most "telling" hit which was made by an Irish graduate of Mr. Spurgeon's college, at the Papists, when he said that in his native country he had seen five hundred of these poor deluded creatures crowd into a hole which wouldn't hold fifty. Yes, brother, open communion, on the part of those who might commune together, *if they would,* does not enable them "to love each other any better for this questionable privilege." Suppose, however, that they try it properly, and then report.

But, in all seriousness, *was* not the Lord's supper instituted "for the purpose of manifesting brotherly love?" When the ordinance is properly observed we feed on Christ. "Take eat; this is my body, which is broken for you." And feeding on the same spiritual food, are we not one in the purest essence, and the most tender and lasting relations? I grant that the result of communion in the right spirit is not so much a "*manifesting*" of brotherly love as a *making* of it, but it is *also* a manifesting, for the best of all reasons—because it is a making. The greater includes the less. So argued Paul, who received his views of communion from the Lord: "The bread which we break, is it not the communion of the body of Christ? For WE, *being many*, are ONE BREAD and ONE BODY, *for we are all partakers of that one bread.*"

"37. *It is a fact* that there is no longer any occasion for maintaining Baptist churches when the true Baptist position in regard to communion as strictly a church ordinance, always to be preceded by baptism, is abandoned; hence it is not surprising that the way from an open-communion Baptist church into a Pedobaptist church, is found exceedingly direct and easy, and that 'many there be which go in thereat.'"

Whately's warning not to press an analogy too far, should be regarded in applying Mr. Foster's quotation to the churches of our brethren, for the gate to which it alludes does not open into a heavenly communion. Indeed, it is better in this case to "leave off before you begin," for it is but a step to "destruction." I have answered this thirty-seventh "fact," in the chapter on Apostolic Example, by saying, that, if it is true, the Baptist denomination ought to die. But I am so much stronger a Baptist than he, or any of my close-communion brethren, that I believe our denomination would have an unimpaired right, aye, and a higher call, to live, if it did not insist on this practice.

If, by anything higher than church authority, the communion is "strictly a church ordinance, always to be preceded by baptism," somebody should arraign the Lord of the supper for instituting it as He did. Was there a Christian church *before the death and resurrection of Christ?* If so, why did He say to Peter, "Thou art πέτρος, and on this rock I WILL BUILD MY CHURCH, and the gates of hell SHALL NOT prevail against it?" The use of the future tense is decisive; and, moreover, Peter was not fit for building till after his restoration from his apostasy. Then, again, where were the other members, the women, who followed Him through Galilee with the twelve, and ministered to him of their substance; and the five hundred brethren who saw Him after He was risen? Was it not in their synagogues that the Master taught, and the disciples listened and worshiped? And why was it that in a Christian church no prayer was made in the name of Christ? He had taught His disciples to pray, but not for His sake. It was after the supper, and under the shadow of Calvary, that He said to them, "*Hitherto* ye have asked nothing in my name; ask, and ye shall receive, that your joy may be full."

But it by no means follows, as is maintained in "A Familiar Dialogue between Peter and Benjamin on the Subject of Close Communion," that the Lord's supper was a Jewish rite, or something belonging to the old dispensation, except in the estimation of those who wish to have everything cut, dried, and labeled, who love neither greenness nor growth, and would have Christianity in the method of its development, and in the precision and importance of its forms, even to the minutest details, a second edition, instead of the spiritual fulfilment, of the Mosaic law. Christ, Himself, as the God-Man, fulfilled the law. While He lived *He was fulfilling it.* He came to be our Passover, and He became our Passover when He offered Himself once and for all. The Jewish passover, which He kept on the eve of its fulfilment in Himself, died in giving birth at His hands to the communion, which, as I hope I have shown in this book, He made a sign and a means of the life which we have in Him, and with each other.

"38. *It is a fact* that whenever persons become unsettled upon the communion question, they become so much unsettled as consistent and steadfast Baptists, and either they, or members of their families, are sooner or later found inside of other than Baptist churches."

Why? Because they are often driven to the conclusion that there is no liberty allowed them to follow their consciences in this regard inside the denomination. This is a question which must soon be settled, if, indeed, by the resolutions of associations the action of individual churches, and the utterances of professedly representative journals, it be not settled already. I scarcely know whether I am a Baptist or not. By Curtis' "Principles and Practices of Baptists," by some of Mr. Foster's "facts," and by the general tone of our Baptist papers, I am not; but if John Bunyan was a Baptist, if Roger Williams was a Baptist; or if Charles Spurgeon, William Brock, or Baptist Noel, is a Baptist, then I am a Baptist too. The decision, however, makes little difference, for no name can be nobler or more appropriate for followers of Christ than that which was given them at Antioch.

"41. *It is a fact* that before the sinner is converted he must give up his determination to have his own way respecting the plan of salvation, and that after his conversion *it does not become him to cling to his own way concerning the duties of religion regardless of the way appointed in the Scriptures.*"

Indisputable. But this resembles what the open communionists think that the close communionists are doing by dogmatizing instead of arguing, and taking for granted, instead of proving, the question at issue. They cannot point to Christ's example, for that is fatal to the idea that "communion is strictly a church ordinance, always to be preceded by baptism;" or to that of the Apostles, or to a single inspired precept, to show that their "way" is "appointed in the Scriptures." When did it begin? On the night of His betrayal, when Christ instituted the communion with only the twelve, before His death, and before His resurrection, which are symbolized by Christian baptism, and before His delivery of the baptismal commission? Or on the day of Pentecost when there was no difference of opinion on the form of water baptism among believers? Or *when Peter withdrew and separated himself from the uncircumcision?* It seems to me that American Baptists must treat Intercommunion as an open question, and recognize the liberty of each church to practise it, or divide into two denominations. Time will tell, and God will use the result for good.

Meanwhile, although honest and kind in discussion, let us call things by their right names. The *Watchman and Reflector*, in apologizing for printing a very mild letter from "the pastor of the largest Baptist church in Philadelphia" (Freedom should make a bow for this heroism), alludes to a nameless contemporary as follows:

"Our views of editorial responsibility do not require us to do in this matter like unto a certain other Baptist editor that we know of; that is, cut out and pare down the language of a correspondent so as to express just what the *liberal minded* editor regards as *proper* to be said. The freedom of such a press—at least among Baptists—is worthy of little less than contempt. The *Watchman* has ever been, and must ever remain, the fearless steadfast defender of the 'faith once delivered' (close communion?), but never by any of the practised arts of suppression, or Jesuitism."

That word has Jesus in it, and it need not be used in this connection even if appropriate. What is it that is here so mildly charged? Suppose that the language of a correspondent who has an opinion of his own on a given subject, and has expressed it clearly, is so changed that a different meaning attaches to the words which are published as his, of what is the author of the change and the publication guilty? Of nothing less than forgery, and that with the intention which is generally the animus of the crime —I mean, *to swindle*; for whoever knowingly publishes as a certain man's utterance something different in meaning from what he has uttered, swindles with ideas instead of notes, and if there is any difference in guilt it may be measured by the difference in value between mind and money. "Charity," which "never faileth," loves fair play, and although she "endureth all things," yet cheating, or unwillingness to hear, especially in the name of her sister, Truth, is something which she finds most grevious to be borne.

In vol. iii. of "The *Baptist* Library, a republication of *Standard Baptist* Works," issued in 1842, and edited by three Baptist ministers, one of whom has no superior in our church as a thinker, a writer, and a scholar, selections from Bunyan and Hall are bound up with Professor Ripley's vindication of close communion, and the "Familiar Dialogue," to which I have already alluded. It is curious, that, in the latter, "*Peter*" is the close communionist, but quite the thing that "Benjamin" cannot answer his arguments, for in a dialogue one of the two must generally play the fool. "Benjamin" was certainly not very bright when it was so easy to "relieve" his "mind" of the suspicion that the Ephesian disciples were "rebaptized." See Appendix (4).

"M." puts the following question to the *Examiner and Chronicle* in its issue of November 19th:

"Is it right, or is it wrong, for a church to receive into its fellowship a brother who declares that while he believes immersion only is baptism, he sees no connection between that ordinance and the supper, and who could sit down at the Lord's table with an unbaptized person without feeling that he had broken a Bible law?"

To which the editor replies as follows:

"We do not see how any regular *Baptist* church could receive a brother holding the views above described. What such a brother needs is to have the way of God more perfectly expounded to him, and he should be commended to the care of some Aquila or Priscilla, kindly to do that service him. If, after such an endeavor, he still persists in seeing no connection between the two ordinances as is believed in by all regular Baptist churches, he should be permitted, as we think, to seek a spiritual home outside the Baptist denomination."

No wonder that Mr. Foster has noticed (see "fact 38") that either those persons who become unsettled upon the communion question, or members of their families, are sooner or later found within other than Baptist churches; for the *Examiner and Chronicle*, and its consituency, which is doubtless large, would make "the Baptist denomination" disagreeable beyond endurance to the former, and keep the latter, if they shared their parents' opinions, from getting into it at all. Unless a different spirit than this prevails, it is clear that "the Baptist denomination" must be divided. Indeed I do not see how Baptist ministers who have publicly denied that water baptism before communion is the divinely appointed order, can remain in their present relations, and keep their manhood, unless they regard such utterances as Dr. Bright's of insufficient representative value. Judged by its merits, it is open to criticism, for it favors a condition of admission to the church which is opposed both to the letter and spirit of the Scriptures. But that it is representative to quite an extent may be safely inferred from the mere fact of its publication. Its author is not likely to be mistaken in a matter like this, for instinct in its sphere is surer than reason.

On close-communion-Baptist principles, nothing but a "thus saith the Lord" is of binding authority. This is a fundamental idea. But where is the Scripture which forbids us to celebrate the Lord's supper either with believers who, in our opinion, have mistaken the mode and subjects of water baptism, or are untouched by the water of the baptismal font? Where is "the body of Christ" limited in its members to Christians who have been dipped in water—except, by implication, in a close-communion-Baptist church? What an Aquila or Priscilla the *Examiner and Chronicle* would have been to show John Bunyan "the better way," or "kindly to do that service" for Robert Hall! I say nothing of the Master and the first communion in this connection, for, though fearless, I would not be irreverent. Even at the meeting of an association in which are some ministers of superior education and large acquaintance with the Scriptures, silence, which is said to give consent, was the only response to a challenge for a precept which shows that the close-communion order is divine. Of course those fearful whispers about the position and the fate of Sunday on close-communion grounds were no answer to Dr. Caswell's question.

Dr. Bright should not bring Aquila and Priscilla into the foreground, for, from the close-communion position, that John's baptism was Christian baptism, and John's preaching Gospel preaching, it does not appear that Apollos needed to have the way of God explained more perfectly, for he understood the baptism of John, and taught diligently the things concerning Jesus. It has been supposed from Acts xviii., 28, that he did not know Jesus as the Messiah until after the teaching of this Christian pair. "The same mistake," says Alford, "has led to the alteration of Ἰησοῦ into the κυρίου of the *rec.*" For it followed that if Apollos did not regard Jesus as the Messiah, he could not have taught diligently the things concerning Him. This author also observes that *the doctrines of the cross*, the resurrection and the outpouring of the Spirit, were unknown to Apollos, "but more particularly the latter, *as connected with Christian baptism.*" It can scarcely be said that Aquila and Priscilla converted Apollos to Christianity, for his face was that way, and he was going thitherward, but they helped him to the goal. One thing, however, is certain, that, *before they instructed him, he held the close-communion view of Johannic baptism;* for, as Meyer remarks, "it is not meant (by 'knowing only the baptism of John') that he was absolutely ignorant *of there being such a thing as Christian baptism, but ignorant of its being anything different from that of John;* he knew, or recognized, in baptism *only that which the baptism of John was:* A SIGN OF REPENTANCE." If it were modest or courteous to follow the example of the *Examiner and Chronicle*, I would suggest that what it needs, in common with many other close communionists, is to be commended to the care of some Aquila or Priscilla, or what would be much better, to study the Scriptures a little more carefully before appealing to them with such confidence as despises the mention of the chapter and verse. We would listen to the Lord.

But potent as may be the say-so of the editor and proprietor of a "*regular*" Baptist weekly, it can scarcely pass for the word of God; and it need not be surprising if some of those who do not like all the tunes which this organ plays, decide to ascertain whether or not they can use the liberty which they have in Christ inside of "the Baptist denomination" before they leave it, or are driven out.

(7.)

Although this book is by no means a review of the various vindications of close communion, it may not be inappropriate in this connection to notice two or three of Mr. Howell's statements in defence of this practice.

In common with those who agree with him, he ignores the difference between believing that dipping in water is essential to communion, and that you are not only bound to observe this prerequisite yourself, but also *to insist that other Christians who interpret the Scriptures differently shall submit to it too, on penalty of exclusion from the Lord's table.* As has been stated, these two things are different, and do not necessarily follow each other. To hold them both involves two conclusions; 1, that the church has power, without an inspired precept, to receive or exclude from the Lord's supper whom she pleases—one which is accepted by the Roman Catholics,—and, 2, that our denomination is the only church, which is just what they claim for theirs.

While settling things to his own satisfaction, and inveighing against the so-called monstrous blunders of Robert Hall, Mr. Howell takes it for granted, notwithstanding many texts to the contrary (see my chapter on "The Baptism of the First Communicants), that the heading of Mark's narrative means that *the baptism of John was the beginning of the Gospel of Jesus Christ.* But every candid scholar must notice that the heading is supplemented by citations from two prophets (Malachi and Isaiah), and that their application to John introduces us to the subject matter of the author. Moreover, "the gospel of Jesus Christ" is here objective, and means *the good news about Him* (see Alford and Meyer *in loc.*), which began, as, it seems to me, Mark's heading asserts, with prophets long anterior to John ; and which, indeed, beamed through God's curse of the serpent into the Eden and the world which sin had blighted : "I will put enmity between thee and the woman, and between thy seed and HER SEED ; it shall bruise thy head, and thou shalt bruise his heel."[1] But the prophecies quoted by Mark are the beginning of the good news about Jesus Christ *in connection with John the Baptist as his forerunner ;* and hence it is that Mark heads and introduces his gospel as he does. Thus Lange, under "Doctrinal and Ethical :" "The Baptist is here, as in the gospel of John., ch. i., *the representative* and *final expression* of the *whole Old Testament.* But the Old Testament itself, *terminating in him,* becomes one great forerunner, and the voice of the Spirit of God in the wilderness, which proclaims the manifestation of Christ ; that is, it becomes a compendious introduction to the original New Testament springing from heaven." So Starke : "Thus the *last messenger of the old covenant* points to the *first of the new.*" So also Gerlach, who speaks of "John's baptism as the *conclusion,* and consequently, also, the

1 Gen. iii., 15 ; see, also, John viii., 42–49, 1 John iii., 8–24.

epitome, of all that the *legal economy* contained in itself." In maintaining that John's ministry belonged to the *Gospel* dispensation, and that John's baptism was *Christian* baptism, Mr. Howell seems to me to maintain essentially that the forerunner *was* the Messiah, and that the Old Testament is the New.

To strengthen a position, the weakness of which, I think, he must have felt, he makes the Baptist say, "Behold the Lamb of God" "*to the multitude*," although there is no such statement in Scripture, and the inference is that the language was addressed to his disciples; for he repeated it "next day" to two of them, one of whom recorded it after all the other Evangelists had written their narratives, and had said nothing about it, although the saying was so remarkable. Had it been part of his public teaching, it would certainly have been mentioned as such by Matthew, Mark, or Luke, for it was a far more wonderful declaration than that which is recorded of him by them all: "The Kingdom of Heaven is at hand." This was appropriate to his mission; and that was not; hence it is to be inferred that it was spoken privately. Moreover, had the words in question been uttered "*to the multitude*," what must they have thought of the Baptist when he sent his disciples to inquire of this same Jesus, "Art thou he that should come, or look we for another?" For it was publicly, and in presence of those who had listened to his preaching, and in all probability had submitted to his baptism,[2] that his messengers propounded his question; for, "*as they departed*, Jesus began to say to the multitudes concerning John, What went YE out to see?"

From such a make-shift as this, and the other, that John baptized in the name of the Coming One (ὁ ἐρχόμενος), it is to be expected that Mr. Howell denies that the disciples whom Paul found at Ephesus were rebaptized, if he does not make Luke, like "Peter" in the "Dialogue," say something altogether different.

Mr. Howell also maintains, that, if John's baptism belonged to the old dispensation, because it was observed before the death and resurrection of Christ, so does the supper; but he surely forgets, first, *that John received his authority to baptize directly from God*, and second, *that Jesus came to His forerunner's baptism after* multitudes had submitted to it, and *before* He had revealed Himself as the Messiah; *while, in person, He instituted the communion, explained its meaning, fixed its formula, and*

[2] Matt. xi., 7; see, also, Luke vii., 29.

enjoined its observance, just before He was led as a lamb to the slaughter.

I know that none but a bigot refuses to tolerate, or fails to respect, honest differences of opinion; but I confess that I find it hard to deal gently with a writer who treats the arguments of such a confessedly gifted and scholarly opponent, so contemptuously, who builds his own on such a sandy foundation, and utters them as if his say-so were fully equivalent to "thus saith the Lord."

(8.)

I notice that Andrew Fuller, in his answer to John Carter, uses the following language: "We verily believe you to be unbaptized, not merely as being only sprinkled, but as receiving it at a time when you could not actively 'put on Christ,' which 'as many as were baptized' in primitive ages did.—Gal. iii., 27."* Now this is not what Paul says; for two words, which are very important, especially in their bearing on Mr. Fuller's assumption that Jesus and the Apostles received *Christian* baptism, are omitted. The text reads, "For *as many of you as* have been baptized INTO CHRIST have put on Christ," and implies, as has

*Complete Works of Rev. Andrew Fuller, Boston, 1833, vol. ii., page 666.

been remarked in this book, that some of the Galatian Christians, like the Romans, and the Ephesian "disciples," had *not* been so baptized. I append a few examples of the meaning of *ὅσοι*, when it is used without qualification, as it is in the two cases of its connection with the baptized:

1. "*As many as* touched were made perfectly whole."—Matt. xiv. 36.

The statement is not that *all* touched the hem of His garment, but that all *who* touched were made perfectly whole; and the implication is that there were some who did not touch, and were not healed.

2. "Neither was there any among them that lacked; for *as many as* were possessed of lands and houses sold them, and brought the prices of the things that were sold and laid them down at the apostles' feet."—Acts iv. 34.

It cannot be denied that this makes a clear distinction between those who had lands or houses, and *those who had not*, unless we hold, that, *because* "*as many of you as* have been baptized into Christ," meant "*you have* ALL been baptized into Christ," Luke intended to tell us that *the primitive Christians* WITHOUT EXCEPTION *owned real estate.* As many as agree to this, and have neither houses nor lands, are yet possessed of valuable *personal* property as surely as consistency is a *jewel.*

3. "For *as many as* have sinned without law shall also perish without law."—Rom. ii. 12.

If this means that *all* had sinned without law, then, in a double sense, the Jews were lawless.

4. "For *as many as* are of the works of the law are under the curse."—Gal. iii., 10.

But those who were of the justification, which is by faith in Christ were neither "of the works of the law," nor "under the curse;" and this was the precise distinction which the Apostle desired to impress upon the foolish Galatians, who had been bewitched, that they should not obey the truth.

5. "But unto you, I say, and unto the rest in Thyatira, *as many as* have not this doctrine, and which have not known the depths of Satan, as they speak; I will put upon you none other burden."—Rev. ii., 24.

The legitimate inference that some of of the Thyatireans *had* this doctrine is made an indisputable fact by the context. That ὅσοι pointed at two parties in the church at Thyatira, is acknowledged and used, as follows, by Mr. Fuller himself, in dissuading a missionary at Serampore from open communion:

"Whoever they were that were thus denominated, it was doubtless some person, or body of persons, that strove to draw off the church from her purity, and to introduce for doctrines the commandments of men· It seems, too, that some of God's servants were seduced by her; good men, whom your plan of admission would have tolerated. And it is worthy of notice that the censure was not directed against her (Jezebel) for doing so, but against the church for suffering it."

But here Mr. Fuller falls into three inaccuracies; first, in saying that the things condemned were mere "doctrines" when the Son of God says, that Jezebel taught and seduced His servants "*to commit fornication, and to eat things sacrificed to idols;*" second, in saying that "the censure is not directed against her," when the Son of God says, "Behold I will cast *her* into a bed, and *them that commit adultery with her* into great tribulation, except they repent of their DEEDS . . . . and I will give untc every one of you according to your WORKS;" and, third, in saying that the censure was "against the *church* for suffering it," when the Son of God addresses himself to the *angel* of the church at Thyatira from the beginning to the end of His message. Whoever the angel was (the name, with *episcopus*, was borrowed from the synagogue, the ruler of which was so called),he had failed in exposing the fornication and idolatry, which Jezebel (whoever she was, or whomsoever she represented), had promoted. Of course the church was also to blame, but, of the two, the rebuke was especially addressed to him. By referring to the last six verses of 1 Cor. vi., it will be seen that fornication on the part of Christians has a double meaning, and is a deeply aggravated sin ; for it is not only against the fornicator's body, but also against Christ, of whom our bodies are members. The Thyatireans who were "*joined unto the Lord,*" and yet followed this seducer, committed *adultery*, for they broke their vows to Him. I confess that it was such gross and glaring misapplications of passages like this to communion with Christians, many of whom were far above me in nearness to Christ, which made me feel that our practice must be wrong when such a defence of it was so common.

In the same letter Mr. Fuller remarks : "To me it appears that pedobaptism opened the door for the Romish apostasy." But this is putting an effect for the cause, if the commonly received opinion among Baptists be correct,—that it was in the heresy of NO SALVATION WITHOUT WATER BAPTISM that pedobaptism began.* "The Romish apostasy" was easy and inevitable when the importance of an outward rite was so awfully overestimated. And who can picture all the apostasies from Christ which owe their origin to this deep seated disposition in man—the blending

* Torrey's Neander, vol. I., page 313.

of superstition and selfishness which expects the kingdom of God to come with observation, and wishes to make the salvation of the soul something far easier, and less subjective, than Jesus declared it to be. For "when He had called the people unto Him, with his disciples also, He said unto them, Whoever will come after Me let him deny himself, and take up his cross, and follow Me."[1] "And if thine eye offend thee, pluck it out, and cast it from thee: it is better for thee to enter into life with one eye rather than having two eyes to be cast into hell-fire."[2]

"Let it be also particularly noticed," says Mr. Fuller, "that our brethren who plead for receiving Christians as Christians RECEIVE THEM TO THE ORDINANCES AS UNDERSTOOD AND PRACTISED BY THEM, and this we do. If the prejudice of a pious Catholic would permit him to request to join with them at the Lord's supper, they would, as we have often been told, receive him, but TO WHAT? Would they provide a wafer for him, and excuse him from drinking of the cup? 'No,' they would say, 'we are willing to receive you to the Lord's supper, in the way we understand and practise it; but we cannot divide the wine from the bread without dispensing with

[1] Mark viii., 34. [2] Matt. xviii., 9.

an essential part of the institution.'" Surely Mr. Fuller knew that there was no essential difference in the manner of observing the Lord's supper among Protestants, that many in every denomination who observed it at all would gladly have partaken with him, if he had not excluded them, and that it was stretching a point to suppose that a Roman Catholic would request to commune with open-communion Baptists unless he had decided to conform to their method for the occasion. I do not see how Mr. Fuller could say, "So do we," of receiving "Christians *as Christians* at the Lord's table, for it was never as such merely, but always as such having been previously dipped in water on profession of their faith in Christ, that his party received each other, and every communicant at the communion. Nay, more, they required membership of good standing in a church of the same faith and order. But I may not understand his argument. Nor is it altogether correct that the open communionists received "Christians as Christians" "to the ordinances, *as understood and practised by them*," for an open communionist may observe the Lord's supper as a baptized person, himself, and yet feel at liberty, and most happy, to sit with his brother who partakes simply as a Christian, or as baptized, although merely sprinkled. Mr. Fuller concludes the paragraph as follows:

"Such is our answer to a pious Pedobaptist. We are willing to receive you to the ordinances of Christ, as we understand and practise them; but we cannot divide the one from the other *without dispensing with an institution of Christ.*"

But instead of showing that Christ so connected the two ordinances that the result mentioned follows necessarily from open communion, Mr. Fuller takes it for granted that the Apostles were not only baptized, but also that their baptism was Christian baptism; and he very skilfully evades the rebaptism of the Ephesian disciples. See my chapter on the Baptism of the First Communicants, and Appendix (4).

On the ground that instrumental music was part of the ceremonial law, which was abrogated by the Messiah, and that there was no authority for such means of praise in the New Testament, Mr. Fuller, like the great majority of the Baptists of his day, and the early English Baptists without exception, was opposed to the use of musical instruments in churches. But there are a great many other things besides our organs, costly as they are, which would be abandoned if the latter principle were strictly applied. I take it that the steeples would come down, with the bells also; that we would worship in upper rooms, or plain meeting-houses, instead of magnificent "churches," some of them costing more than a hundred dollars for every year which has passed since Jesus lay in His borrowed grave; that the baptistery would give place to Nature's fonts, and that dealers in water-proof garments would do a little less business in the ecclesiastical line. I do not say that I am opposed to these things, but simply suggest, that, with others of far greater importance, like Sunday-schools, and missionary societies, for example, they would disappear, if the principle which is so generally received had but a fair application.

Right nobly did this eminent, gifted, and now sainted servant of God, conclude a posthumous publication on the Terms of Communion:

"I am willing to allow that open communion *may* be practised from a conscientious persuasion of its being the mind of Christ; and they ought to allow the same of strict communion; and thus instead of reproaching one another with bigotry on the one hand, or carnal policy on the other, *we should confine our inquiries to the precepts and examples of the New Testament.*"

But he scarcely kept his argument within these limits, for in the same treatise he used the following language:

"If there be no instituted connection between them (baptism and communion) it must go far toward establishing the position of Mr. Bunyan, that 'non-baptism (at least where it arises from error) is no bar to communion.' If Mr. Bunyan's position be tenable, however, *it is rather singular that it should have been so long undiscovered; for it does not appear that such a notion was ever advanced till he or his contemporaries advanced it.* Whatever difference of opinion had subsisted among Christians concerning the mode and subjects of baptism, *I have seen no evidence that baptism was considered by any as unconnected with or unnecessary to the supper.* 'It is certain,' says Dr. Doddridge, 'that as far as our knowledge of primitive antiquity reaches, *no unbaptized person received the Lord's supper.*"

Here the argument is entirely from human authority; but Mr. Fuller has the candor to confess that it must go for nothing if the contrary opinion "be well established from the Scriptures."

I think I have shown in this book that Christian baptism and communion were not connected by their Author as their connection is described in the standards of the churches to-day. It is a fact, too, that the common theory on the subject is repugnant to the instinct, and set aside by the practice, of individual members, and particular congregations, in an increasing degree. In some Pedobaptist churches the invitation to the communion includes all who love the Lord Jesus Christ in sincerity, and in others the profession of His name is added, but left, as I have been informed, to the interpretation of the audience.

There are many Pedobaptists ministers who accept the alleged dependence of communion on previous water baptism as a *church doctrine* rather than as an invariable order of Christ's appointment. That it has been a church doctrine since the time of the earliest fathers, cannot, I suppose, be successfully denied, but so has each of the ideas that the ordinance is invalid unless administered by an ordained minister, and that the bread is the very flesh, and the wine the very blood of the Redeemer. In describing and condemning the heretics of his time, Ignatius, who was contemporaneous with the Apostle John, writes to the Smyrneans as follows:

"They abstain from the eucharist, and from public offices (prayers), because they confess not the eucharist to be the flesh of our Saviour Jesus Christ, which suffered for our sins, and which the Father of His goodness raised again from the dead. And for this cause, contradicting the gift of God, they die in their disputes. But much better would it be for them to receive it, that they might one day rise through it. * * * See that ye all follow your bishop, as Jesus Christ the Father; and the presbytery as the Apostles; and reverence the deacons as the command of God. Let no man do anything of what belongs to the church separately from the bishop. Let that eucharist be looked upon as well established, which is either offered by the bishop, or by him to whom the bishop has given his consent. Wheresoever the bishop shall appear, there let the people (the multitude) be also; as where Jesus Christ is there is the Catholic church. *It is not lawful without the bishop either to baptize or to celebrate the holy communion;* but whatsoever he shall approve of, that is also pleasing unto God; that so whatever is done may be sure and well done."*

It is the bishop, the bishop, throughout his epistles, and quite often in the same style through those of Clement and Polycarp, to say nothing of Barnabas and the Shepherd of Hermas.

Human nature does not take readily to the command of Christ to call no man master; for, instead of serving them, the powerful "exercise dominion" over the weak, which is all the easier, inasmuch as weakness being in admiration and awe of power, and hoping also to benefit by it, loves well to follow it. Hence either the temporal or spiritual authority of an office is so easily increased, that, if it be not constantly limited, it increases itself. Then, too, a multiplication of offices arises on the one hand from the disposition of governing, and, on the other, from that of courting government. The strength and universality of these natural tendencies, and of many others, are amply illustrated in church history.

* The Epistle of St. Ignatius to the Smyrneans, sec. vii. and viii., of Wake's Apostolic Fathers, Phila. reprint, 1846, pp. 115, 116.

For proofs of the genuineness of the Epistles of Ignatius, see "Preliminary Discourse" (*Ibid.* p. 83).

Was it not likely, I had almost said inevitable, that the influence of Judaism in the early churches would show itself in making too much of an initiatory rite from a too close connection of it with the benefits of the system to which it belonged? We know what havoc of the peace and spirituality of primitive Christendom was made by the overestimate of the claims of circumcision. The same disposition, taken into the new dispensation, and at length giving up the old rite, would naturally fasten on one of the two Christian ordinances as initiatory in the Jewish sense. Indeed, when we consider that the idea that water baptism is the only medium of saving grace, can be traced as a church doctrine almost to the apostolic age, we need be less surprised at its subsequent unvarying connection with the supper; for if it appeared proper that a man should commune *as saved by Christ, and thus only;* and also that *salvation was impossible except by water baptism,* the latter was necessarily required before the former was allowed. But as a totally different idea obtains among the mass of Protestants, it is not strange that in the absence of any precept making water baptism a prerequisite of the Lord's supper, the practice of open communion is increasing, and the desire for it still more so.

But open communion will be enjoyed by only those who feel that it is a liberty and a blessing, which they have in Christ. Mr. Fuller tried it, but not being sure of its propriety, he failed to experience that benefit which would have led him to make a custom of his experiment, the making and result of which he confesses as follows: "So far have I been from indulging a sectarian or party spirit, that my desire for communion with all who are friendly to the Saviour has in one instance led me practically to deviate from my general sentiments on the subject; the reflection on which, however, having afforded me no satisfaction, I do not intend to repeat it." As it was *a practical deviation from his general sentiments*, it could not be a vehicle of grace and joy, for "he that doubteth is damned if he eat;" that is, he is condemned by his own conscience. But if the act had been spontaneous and untrammelled, an expression of that perfect love which casteth out fear, then, in communion with Christ, this beloved disciple would have felt his union with his Christian kindred, who were receiving the same spiritual life from the same divine source—that heavenly experience of which the members of the family, who are yet pilgrims, have but foretastes on the homeward way.

(9.)

In a recent sermon entitled "Baptism before Communion," by Rev. A. J. F. Behrends, he remarks of the latter: "It is the Lord's table *spread by and under the protection of the church.* In the very act of spreading the table, she claims to judge upon the qualifications of the applicants, else what right has she to touch these emblems with one of her fingers?" But can she alter the qualifications indicated by the Lord, or differ about them at different times, without proving, as Protestants profess to hold, and Baptists most of all, that she is fallible, and that it is well for her, and the world, that HE is King in Zion? But *what is the church* which is thus held up as the spreader, the guardian, and the judge of the LORD'S table? The Roman Catholic, which of all existing Christian organizations is at once the largest and most ancient? Mr. Behrends would promptly answer "No;" for, believing itself to be "the church," and to possess the power which he ascribes to "the church," it recognizes sprinkling as baptism, an infant as a proper subject, and gives one of the elements to the laity thus sprinkled in infancy.

If we suggest the Presbyterian, his response must still be in the negative, for it, too, changing both the mode and subjects of baptism, maintains, in his opinion, a communion of the unbaptized. It is clear that it is neither the invisible church, nor the aggregate of Christian churches, but the Baptist church, and the Baptist church only, which, in the logic of the close-communion view, spreads, protects, and controls, the table of the LORD.

Depend upon it that it is not

PRIVATE INTERPRETATION,

AND

OPEN COMMUNION,

which is printed on the ticket for "the express train that stops at no station this side of Rome;" but

THE CHURCH, THE CHURCH,

AND

CLOSE COMMUNION;

and it is a matter of little consequence whether one purchases at an Episcopal, or a Baptist, at a Methodist, or a Presbyterian office, for under different names the track is the same, and, whether or not it leads to Rome, it is the Roman road. Churchism in the Roman Catholic sense is growing in parts of almost all the Protestant churches, and is struggling with the true Protestant element. It is one thing to believe in "the church," and quite another to feel that it is your church, and yours only.

"Cyprian," says Mr. Behrends, "refused to administer baptism to an applicant who had received baptism at the hands of heretics—which was considered irregular and invalid—because the man had repeatedly partaken of the supper; an evidence that the church of that day looked upon baptism subsequent to the supper as an incongruity and contradiction." But we Baptists who often baptize Christians who have partaken of the communion for years in other churches, must either think that it is not the Lord's supper which they celebrate, or differ widely from Cyprian. He thought that communion had so ratified the baptism of this man, that its repetition would be improper, although in itself he regarded it as null and void. "Baptism at the hands of heretics" was a subject on which Christendom was profoundly agitated and clearly divided, before Cyprian's time. But the discussion was renewed, and hotly pressed, while he was bishop of Carthage. He held Tertullian's view in opposition to the Roman see, and to the Western churches in general. If a converted heretic came to the church at Rome, he was received as a baptized Christian, and confirmed by the bishop. It was therefore by only a party that "baptism at the hand of heretics" was considered "irregular and invalid," and hence no action based on this idea can properly be predicated of "the church of that day."

The case to which Mr. Behrends alludes is thus recorded in Neander's History of the Christian Religion :*

"There was in the church of Alexandria a converted heretic who lived as a member of the church for many years, and participated in the various acts of worship. Happening once to be present at a baptism of catechumens, he remembered that the baptism which he himself had received in the sect from which he was converted (probably a Gnostic sect), bore no resemblance whatever to the one he now witnessed. Had he been aware that whoever possesses Christ in faith, possesses all that is necessary to his growth in grace, and to the salvation of his soul, this circumstance could not have given him so much uneasiness. But as this was not so clear to him, he doubted as to his title to consider himself a real Christian, and fell into the greatest distress and anxiety, believing himself to be without baptism, and the grace of baptism. In tears he threw himself at the bishop's feet and besought him for baptism. The bishop endeavored to quiet his fears ; he assured him that he could not, at this late period, after he had so long partaken of the body and blood of the Lord, be baptized anew. It was sufficient that he had lived for so long a time in the fellowship of the church, and all he had to do was to approach the holy sup-

* Torrey's Neander, vol. i., page 323.

per with unwavering faith and a good conscience. But the disquieted man found it impossible to overcome his scruples and regain his tranquillity. So destructive to peace of conscience were the effects of such tenacious adherence to outward things, of not knowing how to rise with freedom to those things of the spirit which the inward man apprehends by faith."

Cyprian believed that the God of the heretics (some of whom may have been Baptists) was not the true God, and that their Christ was not the true Christ; hence that their baptism was nothing. This position he defended with all his energy, and bated not a jot, although he was opposed by Stephanus of Rome, who excommunicated the bishops of Asia Minor, Cappadocia, Galatia, and Cilicia, as Anabaptists. Yet so considerate of circumstances was Cyprian, and so free to shape his course acordingly, that he actually exhorted this man, *whom he considered unbaptized*, to "*approach the holy supper with unwavering faith and a good conscience.*" Thus, in one case, at least, and against greater difficulties than prevent Mr. Behrends from following his example, Cyprian was an open communionist.

But why not mention other points of difference between Cyprian and the ninteenth-century Baptists in America, or say something of what would surely be called the popish superstitions of "the church of that day," so that the people may judge of the value of its authority, and of his on the subject in hand? His defence of the *clinici* was certainly liberal for him, but probably it was made because they were inside of "the church." Said he:

"The breast of the believer is washed, the soul of man is cleansed, by the merits of faith. In the sacraments of salvation, where necessity compels and God gives permission, the divine thing, *though outwardly abridged, bestows all that it implies on the faithful.* Or if any one supposes that they have obtained nothing because they have been merely *sprinkled* with the water of salvation, they must not be so deceived themselves, as to think that they ought therefore to be baptized over again, in case they recover from their sickness. But if those who have once been consecrated by the baptism *of the church,* cannot again be baptized, why fill them with perplexity in regard to their faith and the grace of the Lord."*

This bishop distinguished between the outward and the inward when it suited him, and when it was otherwise he confounded them. Much closer to apostolical times, we find Clement of Rome, supposed to be St. Peter's successor, so thoroughly convinced that the phœnix revived from its own ashes as to use it in proof of the Christian doctrine of the resurrection;† an argument which was repeated by Tertullian, Origen, Cyril, and the generality of the ancient fathers.

* Torrey's Neander, vol. i. p. 310.

† Jun. Notae in Clem. p. 34, Wake's Apostolic Fathers, p. 89.

Ignatius, whose writings were preserved by his friend and fellow-martyr, Polycarp, both of whom are supposed to have been disciples of the Apostle John, wrote to the Tralleans that they were all to reverence the deacons as Jesus Christ, the bishop as the Father, and the presbytery as the sanhedrim of God, and the college of the Apostles; and that without these (three orders) *there was no church.** If a volume of the opinions of the fathers, which they felt and showed as convictions, could but be placed in the hands of our deacons, and read aloud at our social meetings, it might increase their interest, and be a means of grace in convincing many credulous worshippers of the fancied heroes of a falsely pictured past, that, after all, the Master is the best Teacher, that His word is the only standard, and that private interpretation is at once an inalienable Christian right, and an essential condition of the reign of Truth. Far be it from me to speak lightly of the glorious company of the early confessors and martyrs, but I cannot forget what makes their glory all the brighter, that they were fallible, like us, that they were influenced by their surroundings, and that they were the subjects of many and conflicting notions, which most of us would ridicule as vagaries, or lament as delusions. It has been boldly but

* Wake's Apostolic Fathers, p. 102.

truly said that the further back we go in the Christian era toward the Apostles, the more ignorance we find of the Scriptures ; and, it may be added, the stronger tendency to superstition, and the closer connection between forms and saving grace.

No matter what has been thought or done since Christ ascended, it is never by divine right that "the church," or any of the churches, takes the Lord's supper out of His hands, who is at once its Author and its Subject, and conditions it as it was not conditioned by Him. I have tried to show that if either His example, or Paul's teaching, were followed, believers would feel at home, and be welcomed, at this memorial of their one and only Saviour in whatever church they found it. And I hope that the time is coming when Christians of every name, still holding many differences, will rejoice to hold this ordinance as they receive their life from Christ, in common—as theirs because it is His, and His because it is theirs. But if we cannot thus agree, yet the truth which might be so beautifully symbolized remains forever—that we who receive Him are one family, heirs of God and joint heirs with Christ, and that we are going home together through the same difficulties, and with the same help, to our "inheritance which is incorruptible, and undefiled, and that fadeth not away."

www.ingramcontent.com/pod-product-compliance
Lightning Source LLC
LaVergne TN
LVHW011237110826
845150LV00006B/1664

* 9 7 8 1 4 2 5 5 1 4 3 4 1 *